# Teaching Large Classes
## Usable Practices from Around the World

*Edited by*

### Mary Cherian
National Institute of Education, Nanyang Technological University, Singapore

### Rosalind Y. Mau
National Institute of Education, Nanyang Technological University, Singapore

Singapore • Boston • Burr Ridge, IL • Dubuque, IA • Madison, WI • New York • San Francisco
St. Louis • Bangkok • Bogotá • Caracas • Kuala Lumpur • Lisbon • London • Madrid
Mexico City • Milan • Montreal • New Delhi • Santiago • Seoul • Sydney • Taipei • Toronto

# McGraw-Hill Education

A Division of The McGraw-Hill Companies

**Teaching Large Classes**
Usable Practices from Around the World

1 2 3 4 5 6 7 8 9 10 GW ANL 06 05 04 03 02

**When ordering this title, use ISBN 0-07-120280-3**

Printed in Singapore

# Contents

# Prologue

*Mary Cherian and Rosalind Y. Mau*

Large classes are a relatively new phenomenon. After all, until a few decades ago, formal education was available only to the elite. Formal education developed in Asia and Europe as far back as 3,000 B.C. and there have been periods such as the Golden Age of Greece when education was widespread (Michael, n.d.). However, it was only in the 19th Century that education for all became a priority. By the middle of the 20th Century, it was no more acceptable to consider education as a privilege for a few. Instead, education for all became a matter of social justice and equity. Societies across the world began to see that all children—regardless of gender, race and social class— should enjoy the privilege of going to school. In 1948, this sentiment was embodied in Article 26, the Right to Education, of the Universal Declaration of Human Rights (United Nations, 1948). Education was now elevated to the status of an individual right.

Increasingly, education was seen also as a very worthwhile investment in the economy of a country (Power, 1995). Then, after the Cold War, the emphasis moved beyond investing in the economy to promoting social cohesion and democratic participation (UNESCO, 1996). But the challenge remains the same: to reach and educate as many as possible and to improve the quality of education (UNESCO, 1995). Large classes are a direct outcome of our efforts to use limited resources to reach and educate as many as possible. Today, large classes are the norm in many parts of the world. We hear of classes of all levels that have 40, 60 or even more students. Experienced teachers tell us that good teaching and learning can take place in these large classes. Such teachers' insights are shared in the chapters that follow.

# By-passing the Class-size Debate

When the topic of large classes is mentioned, the conversation often swings to the issue of ideal class size. It becomes a large-versus-small debate. This on-going debate has the assumption that teaching and learning are likely to be better in smaller classes than in larger ones (Achilles, 1997; Nye, 1992; Wenglinsky, 1997). You are probably familiar with research supporting such preferences. However, other research has been inconclusive (Costello, 1992; Hargreaves, Galton & Pell, 1997; Litke, 1995; Picus, 2000; Pritchard, 1999). The perception of the 'largeness' of the class—and in turn, perceptions of 'crowdedness'—are strongly coloured by how accustomed the teachers and students are to densely populated settings. For those who are comfortable in large groups, class size may not be an issue at all. For instance, ethnographic studies in Japan and China revealed that these teachers saw little relationship between class size and learning outcomes (Biggs, 1999; Jin & Cortazzi, 1999).

In a recent study of mathematics achievement and class size in nine countries, Pong & Pallas (2001) discovered that only in the United States were smaller classes found to be better for mathematics achievement. They speculated that in America, class size may influence learning outcomes because class size is a real issue and the American public believes that small classes are better. Just being convinced that something is better than something else can influence what happens in each case. They went on to say that "regardless of the likelihood of this interpretation, we hope we have illustrated the perils of generalizing research findings from the United States to other countries" (pp. 270).

Because there are so many factors involved, direct comparisons that result in sweeping statements can be very misleading. And for the kind of journey that this book invites you to take, such direct comparisons serve little purpose. We believe there are unique strengths and limitations to every class size. There are many usable strategies to reach and teach students in classes of all sizes. But in this book, we focus on discovering more about large classes of 40 or more students. In so doing, *Teaching Large Classes* by-passes the debate on class size and speaks to the current reality that large classes are what millions of teachers and students experience in many regions of the world.

At this point, we would like to caution that one should not jump to conclusions that larger classes are better either. Our stand is that singling out one dimension of classes (class size) and pitting two extremes against each other (large versus small) may not only be futile but may also make us less open to discoveries about teaching and learning within classrooms that do not fit our stereotypes of ideal settings. For instance, Pradnya Patet and Meera Oke (chap. 3) surface advantages large classes offer for constructivist teaching. Like them, the other authors offer new perspectives from their unique standpoints.

## Experiencing Large Classes

For teachers in developing countries, this book offers much-needed examples of practices in non-Western, less affluent and more crowded parts of the world. The first three chapters transport you into the classrooms of rural villages and townships in South Africa as well as large cities such as Beijing in China and Mumbai in India. A basic premise here is that the experience of a large class is qualitatively different for students growing up in densely populated places. As compared to students in less crowded regions, these students are accustomed to large groups of people.

Chapter 4 on the Waldorf Schools, the world's largest independent school movement, introduces an alternative, highly successful approach. Waldorf principles are illustrated using classroom scenes from African nations. Chapter 5 gives a rich description of two whole-school transformations in Israel. Chapter 6 describes three pilot projects spanning two decades and three continents. In this chapter, Jessica Ball shares the exciting progression of her work that first involved Malays, Iban and Dayaks in Malaysia and then, First Nations, Inuits, Aleut and Metis groups in Canada and now, groups in 11 African nations.

The value of inclusiveness permeates all chapters and is crystalised in Chapter 7 on children with disabilities. In the following chapter, the focus shifts to highly able children. The next three chapters cover teacher-student relationships (chap. 9), cooperative learning (chap. 10) and authentic assessments through student portfolios (chap. 11). Teacher-student relationships are a recurring theme in several chapters. Similarly, cooperative learning has become such an indispensable part of large-class teaching in many parts of the world that we felt the need for a chapter on it. We include a chapter on student portfolios because it is a form of authentic assessment that has the potential to directly enhance the teacher's capacity to meet the needs of diverse students in large classes.

The chapters have come to us from around the world. In some cases, co-authors live in different countries. Thus, as *Teaching Large Classes* was taking form, the manuscript traveled thousands of miles by air, road and electronic mail. But there was one road that this manuscript was on more than any other: The Pan-Island Expressway (PIE) in Singapore. To get to our university campus from our homes, both Mary Cherian and Rosalind Mau used this expressway. First the acquisitions editor and later the senior editor, typesetter and others from McGraw-Hill drove over on it to meet with us. Reading this book may be likened to cruising along the PIE.

## Cruising through Teaching Large Classes

If you were to arrive at our airport, get into a taxi and head for our campus, you would travel on the PIE from one end of the island to the other. It would be a smooth and mostly uninterrupted journey, giving you time to take in passing scenes. The first few miles of the expressway are lined with flowering shrubs and carefully pruned trees. Clusters of high-rise apartment complexes stand on both sides. Now and then, a school would come into view. You would also see 'flatted' factories (factories housed in high rise buildings with each factory occupying a storey or two). Such buildings continue to be present but they become less visible from the second half of the expressway. The foliage becomes denser: older trees laden with a variety of ferns and climbers; slopes of giant ferns and stretches of forested thickets.

Sitting in the taxi, you can only guess what it feels like to be living in one of the apartment complexes, to be working in a flatted factory or trekking through a thicket. However, with a little encouragement from you, your taxi driver may volunteer information about these settings by describing them and sharing stories of day-to-day life in these parts. It would still not be the same as being there yourself. But it would be better than if you were to make sense of all you saw along the PIE by relying solely on your own understandings and experiences of another place. Similarly, as you cruise from one setting to the next in this book, allow the chapter authors to help you develop a deeper understanding of large-class teaching in the settings described. Our hope is that you will connect with what is being described, reflect on the authors' insights and, thus, move forward in your understanding of teaching and learning.

Each of our authors is either an experienced teacher or teacher educator who has something significant to add to our understanding of large-class teaching. They are passionate about their ideals and, at the same time, are deeply appreciative of good teaching practices within the local contexts they describe. At the end of every chapter, you will find more information about the author(s). Several of them have lived and worked in three or more regions of the world. With such international perspectives forming the backdrop, this book is a unique collection of scenes from classrooms in various countries— glimpses carefully selected and shared with the conviction that we have much to learn from peoples everywhere.

# References

Achilles, C. M. (1997). Small classes, big possibilities. *The School Administrator, 54*(9), 6-9, 12-13, 15.

Biggs, J. (1999). Learning from the Confucian heritage: So size doesn't matter? *International Journal of Educational Research, 29*, 723-738.

Costello, P. A. (1992). *The effectiveness of class size on reading achievement.* (ERIC Document Reproduction Service No. ED 400035).

Hargreaves, L., Galton, M., & Pell, A. (1997, March). *The effects of major changes in class size on teacher-pupil interaction in elementary school classes in England: Does research merely confirm the obvious?* Paper presented at the American Educational Research Association Annual Conference, Chicago. (ERIC Document Reproduction Service No. ED 409123).

Jin, L., & Cortazzi, M. (1999). Dimensions of dialogue: Large classes in China. *International Journal of Educational Research, 29*, 739-761.

Litke, R. A. (1995). *Learning lessons from large classes: Student attitudes toward effective and ineffective methods in large classes.* (ERIC Document Reproduction Service No. ED 384088).

Michael, P. (n.d.). *From Socrates to Miss Crabtree: Teaching through the ages.* Retrieved February 27, 2002, from http://www.riverofwords.org/history.html.

Nye, B. A (1992). *The lasting benefits study. A continuing analysis of the effect of small class size in kindergarten through third grade on student achievement test scores in subsequent grade levels: Fifth grade.* Technical Report. (ERIC Document Reproduction Service No. ED 35499).

Picus, L. (2000). *In search of more productive schools: A guide to resource allocation in education.* Eugene, OR: ERIC Clearinghouse on Educational Management. Retrieved March 25, 2002 from http://eric.uoregon.edu/hot_topics/class_size.html.

Pong, S., & Pallas, A. (2001). Class size and eighth-grade math achievement in the United States and abroad. *Educational evaluation and policy analysis, 23*(3), 251-273.

Power, C.N. (1995). *Preface of '50 years for education'*. Retrieved on March 2, 2002, from http://www.unesco.org/education/educprog/50y/brochure/pref. htm.

Pritchard, I. (1999). *Reducing class size: What do we know?* Office of Educational Research and Improvement, U.S. Department of Education. National Institute on Student Achievement, Curriculum and Assessment (SAI 98-3027).

UNESCO (1995). *50 years of education.* Paris: Author. Retrieved March 2, 2002, from http://www.unesco.org/education/educprog/50y/brochure.htm..

UNESCO (1996). *Learning: The treasure within.* Report of the International Commission on Education for the Twenty-first Century. Paris: Author.

United Nations (1948). *Universal declaration of human rights.* Geneva, Switzerland: Author.

Wenglinsky, H. (1997). *When money matters: How educational expenditures improve student performance and how they don't.* Princeton, NJ: The Educational Testing Service, Policy Information Center.

# CHAPTER 1

# Transforming Large-class Teaching in South Africa

*Bill Holderness*

My introduction to large classes and to seriously overcrowded class-rooms occurred 20 years ago in South Africa. As an education lecturer at the local university, I was invited by the Department of Education to join an inspection panel. The purpose of our visit was to assess progress in primary schools involved in the first year of a Primary Education Upgrading Programme (PEUP). We set ourselves the task of visiting 114 schools during that month—most of them spread out across what is now the North West Province, on the southern edge of the Kalahari Desert.

During that month, I became aware of the classroom realities that face teachers of large classes in township and remote rural schools. The damaging socio-economic and educational consequences of the South African minority government's apartheid policy were starkly evident during these visits. In village after village, we found many instances of schools with disempowered and demoralised teachers, occupying overcrowded and under-resourced classrooms in badly neglected school buildings. Marginalised, illiterate and desperately impoverished communities generally surrounded these schools. The condition and circumstances of such teaching and learning environments would have been considered totally unacceptable for 'white' children living in towns or farmhouses.

## Experiencing Large Classes

For the next 15 years, I was deeply involved in the efforts of the PEUP, as a researcher and later co-ordinator. This gave me the opportunity to become intimately acquainted with the challenges of large-class teaching and it is on these insights that much of this chapter is based. Exposure to related socio-political issues continued in subsequent years when I served as provincial convenor and national evaluator of the Thousand Schools Project. The chief purpose of the project was to identify and improve the 1,000 'neediest' schools in South Africa.

## Two Snapshots

To establish shared points of reference in the PEUP, we begin by visiting the first 2 schools on our 'inspection list'. Each of them was on the outskirts of Mafikeng, the small provincial capital, which was to become my home for the next 15 years.

The first 'school' was in an informal settlement on the northern side of the town. It was built of loose, corrugated iron sheets. Here, within a temporary iron shack, 70 children sheltered from the sun in a single room. There were no tables and chairs—only a few long benches. Instead of books and writing utensils, there were a few slates and for the rest, sandy ground upon which to practise writing and doing basic mathematical operations. Because this was a double-session 'school', at noon, under the blazing October midday sun, a new class of similar size began its afternoon classes in the same environment. Not surprisingly, the teacher did not know the names of more than a handful of pupils.

The following day, we visited a state primary school on the western side of town. Here we found 124 and 125 children respectively in the two 1st-grade classrooms. The third of the 1st-grade classes was limited to only 50 children—the reason for which will be considered later.

## Elsewhere in Africa

Similar, if not worse, conditions can be found in other parts of the world. The recent Oxfam Education Report (Watkins, 2000) acknowledges that it is not uncommon, especially in urban areas, for teachers to be instructing classes of more than 100 children. In Tanzania, for example, an additional 34,223 classrooms will be needed to reduce the average class size from the current level of 75 to a maximum of 40 per class. Official statistics often obscure the gravity of the situation. What is clear is that large classes are with us for years time to come and cannot be simply wished away.

*Children Not Yet in School*   To make matters worse, there are still large numbers of children out of school. The United Nations Children's Fund (UNICEF, 1998) estimated the global figure at 135 million in 1995 while the United Nations Educational, Scientific and Cultural Organisation's World Education Report (UNESCO, 1998) put the figure for the same year at 145 million. Global estimates such as these are as good as the national reporting systems on which they are based and these systems are notoriously weak (Watkins, 2000). In terms of enrolment levels, sub-Saharan Africa faces the most severe problems. The gap between population-growth rate and enrolment-growth rate left 2 million more African children out of school in 1995 than in 1990. That figure is expected to rise by a further 9 million during the period 1995 to 2015. In all other developing regions of the world, however, there is a continuing decline in the number of children out of school.

At present, about 12% of all the 6- to 11-year-old children in the world live in Africa. By 2005, their share in the total number out of school will have risen to just under a half, and by 2015, 3 out of every 4 children of primary-school age not in school will live in Africa. Thus, whilst many children in Africa will experience an inferior quality of education in overcrowded classes, large sections of the population will even be denied the opportunity of ever entering a primary school. Failure to provide an education deepens the level of poverty and reinforces the degree of marginalisation from international trade.

***Effects of HIV/AIDS*** The problem of coping with large numbers of learners is further aggravated by the rapidly growing incidence of HIV/AIDS infection amongst teachers. In many African countries, the teaching profession is being devastated by the pandemic. Infection rates of up to 40% have been reported from Zambia and Malawi. In 1999, AIDS-related illnesses were estimated to have claimed the lives of more than 1,000 teachers in Zambia, which is double the number of 3 years earlier. In some countries, these deaths outstrip the number of graduates emerging from that country's teacher education institutions.

In some of the worst affected countries, such as Zambia and Malawi, it is estimated that almost one third of the children have lost one or both parents through HIV/AIDS. Many of these children are then cared for by relatives who themselves lack the resources to send a child to school. In South Africa, it is increasingly common for children to be responsible for raising their younger siblings whilst caring for sick and dying adults. The existence of these child-headed households has significant implications for teachers of large classes (Holderness, 2001). For example, new ways of supervising homework and of involving sibling caregivers in the education of children will need to be considered.

# Improving Teaching through Factors Affecting Quality

Since human and physical resources are limited in South Africa, the notion of creative large-class teaching at schools needs to be developed. One of the emphases of my chapter is that improvement in the quality of teaching in large classes depends on a number of inter-related factors. The physical state of the *school building*, the *classroom environments* and the availability of *learning materials* can all strongly influence the extent to which an educator can function efficiently, effectively and enthusiastically.

*Learning Materials*    It is for this reason that the Primary Education Upgrading Programme (referred to above) directed the initial 'upgrading efforts' of schools at improving the classroom environments and engaging the local school communities in this process. It also directed much of its time and effort into developing and disseminating appropriate learning materials. Much of this was achieved through holding writers' workshops with local teachers and teacher educators. The resulting Handbooks for Teachers ultimately served as cross-curricular guides at all levels of primary schooling (e.g. Holderness, 1992; Holdernes, 1993). Teachers of large classes who joined the programme for the first time were coached in the use of these materials when they attended the locally run in-service courses.

*Lesson Planning and Preparation*    Through the locally-run in-service courses, teachers learnt the importance of being well organised *before* the teaching day began. This entailed making learning apparatus (often with the help of children or community members) and having these set out in 'shoe boxes' for distribution by the group leaders. Whilst the class was busy with these occupational tasks, the teacher would teach groups in turn at the front of the class.

The recommended arrangement that worked effectively in many lessons (particularly languages and mathematics) was to have five groups, each with 10 members. Depending on the subject matter, the basis for grouping was ability, mixed-ability or social. With support from in-service courses and teaching materials, teachers soon learnt how to effectively manage one-hour lessons. During that time, they could teach each group at the front for about 7 minutes (at a level appropriate to that group). Having sent the group back to their desks with an application task clearly explained, the teacher would then spend a few minutes walking around, checking on the progress of the other four groups.

In language lessons in particular, children needed to have their work checked or they wished to read out what they had written to an adult. To avoid children wasting time in queues, other teachers, the principal or even literate parents would enjoy coming to the class to help listen to and check the children's work. By such means, teachers were able to spend more time concentrating on the task of teaching, and pupils on the job of learning—rather than queuing.

By contrast I recall observing a 'teacher-centred' lesson in a nearby school in which the teacher spent the first 15 minutes of the period handing out to each pupil in turn a yellow crayon (to draw the sun), a green crayon (to draw a hill) and a blue crayon (to colour the sky). After the children had copied the picture from the blackboard, she spent the last 10 minutes of the period collecting each of the crayons in turn from the pupils. She had not yet learnt what the PEUP endeavoured to teach, namely that in a learner-centred classroom, certain responsibilities should be delegated to the children.

## Responding to the Class Size Challenge

Let us now return to our school on the outskirts of Mafikeng and see how the issue of class size was worked out in practice.

Why did the school described in section 2 have 1st-grade enrolments of 124, 125 and then one of only 50 learners? Although evidence on the relationship between class size and education performance is inconclusive, our programme recognized that *exceptionally large class sizes* could seriously inhibit the quality of educational provision. Given the physical architecture of the average classroom, the PEUP set a firm condition for school participation: in order to participate in the reform programme (PEUP), a class had to meet the requirement of having *no more than 50 learners*. On this occasion, as members of the inspection panel, we were asked if the number of pupils could be spread more evenly to 66 children per class. In so doing, we might allow all three 1st-grade teachers to be included in the programme and, thus, start practising the new 'child-centred, activity-based, problem-solving approaches' we were advocating.

This request posed a typical dilemma for the panel. In fairness to the children, should we compromise on our insistence upon 50 as a maximum enrolment for a PEUP class? But would that be fair to the teacher who was trying to introduce new teaching methods and learning materials designed for a maximum class size of 50 pupils? We decided, correctly as it turned out, that we would have to be cruel to be kind.

We maintained it would be impossible for any teacher to be expected to use learner-centred approaches with more than 50 children in a class. Furthermore, the intended benefits of the PEUP intervention would be nullified and at best diluted. Indeed, an attempt to implement PEUP-approaches in such large classes would, we believed, be inappropriate and probably detrimental to the education of the children and to the professional well being of the teachers.

Therefore, it was a relief to find, less than a year later, that the local community had met with the school teachers and departmental officials and initiated the building and equipping of additional classrooms. Three years later, this school became one of the PEUP's leading schools, and took upon itself the job of inspiring neighbouring schools to do likewise and to transform their classroom environments.

## Resilient, Resourceful Teachers

As we moved around from school to school in subsequent years, what struck us was the resilience of these poor communities and the noticeable spark of enthusiasm and hope that had recently been kindled at least amongst the 1st-grade teachers. Almost without exception, the principals and junior primary teachers of the schools warmly received us. For many remote rural schools, this was the first visit by members of the education department for at least 15 years. In breaking the isolation of these schools, and by putting neighbouring schools in contact with each other, new possibilities were suddenly created.

Encouraged by the Department of Education, the teachers of large classes from the different schools began to meet each other on a fairly regular basis. They would visit each other's classes and teach exemplary lessons. From this process of sharing and mutual support, a fresh surge of optimism and confidence was generated.

## Transforming Classrooms

In many cases, previously dreary and disorganised classrooms became transformed into organised and attractive places of learning. Learners and parent community members often participated in the 'spring-cleaning' exercise. Walls were painted, furniture repaired and broken window panes replaced. Local village carpenters made shelves along the walls, on which could be stored cardboard shoeboxes, holding teacher-made work-cards and occupational tasks. Below these shelves were usually 50 individual lockers, wherein each child could store his lunch box and exercise books. An interest table, reading corner and cardboard shop were often set up in such classrooms.

*We saw how professionally empowering it is when teachers mutually reinforce each other over a period of time. We saw how effectively teachers could transform their drab and dreary classrooms into stimulating places of learning and convert waste materials into useful learning aids.*

By contrast with the tin-shack classroom described above, this was a learning environment conducive to learning—and one in which individual children felt a sense of belonging, ownership and shared responsibility. Each child could see his name displayed on a locker, birthday chart and duty list; he had his own desk and chair to occupy; he belonged to a small group of learners when engaged in various cooperative learning tasks. Yet, here he was in a class of 50 children—just as many as had been sitting in rows on long benches in the tin shack. But now he felt he was at a 'real school'; he had a good chance of succeeding, and of being recognised and acknowledged by his teacher.

## Emerging Local Trainers

From amongst the ranks of the local educators, exemplary teachers began to emerge as leaders. In subsequent years, they were elected into district teams for each class level. These groups soon took responsibility for organising in-service workshops each year in their districts. They demonstrated new teaching strategies in their classrooms whilst teachers from neighbouring schools stood and observed from along the sides and back of the room. Immediately thereafter, the observing teachers were given the opportunity to practise the 'new methods'. The 50 learners then took their chairs outside and sat in 10 small groups (each with 5 pupils). This provided the opportunity for each observing teacher—*and her school principal*—to try out and gain confidence using the new teaching approaches and materials.

*From amongst the ranks of the local educators, exemplary teachers began to emerge as leaders. They demonstrated new teaching strategies in their classrooms whilst teachers from neighbouring schools stood and observed from along the sides and back of the room. Immediately thereafter, the observing teachers were given the opportunity to practise the 'new methods'.*

Such workshops lasted for a few days and were held twice a year. To support teachers who joined the education upgrading programme for the first time, and to provide reinforcement for those who were trying to implement the improvements in their large classes, these workshops were repeated each year. Thus, camaraderie was built up amongst the teachers, where previously they had been working in isolation, often separated by great distances and not exposed to any new approaches. Now teachers were able to look forward each year to a fresh round of workshops and might themselves take responsibility for presenting sections of a workshop.

This inexpensive and locally organised provision of school-based in-service workshops was empowering and inexpensive to maintain. It received acclaim from a number of researchers. Thompson (author of the authoritative book, *Education and Development in Africa*) claimed that no other country in the world had ever come so close to providing in-service training for primary school teachers on a permanent, rolling-on basis (Holderness, 1986). Whilst previously the burden of teaching large classes had seemed overwhelming, now there was a collegial support system for teachers to improve the quality of their teaching.

## Widespread Take-up

In the years that followed, growing numbers of schools with large classes became involved in the PEUP. Eventually, after 15 years, all the 940 eligible primary schools were at least theoretically involved in this self-help, school improvement initiative. These schools were spread out across a vast area of some 1,200 kilometres from Moretele (north of Pretoria) to Thaba'Nchu (near Bloemfontein). This area— previously known as the homeland of Bophuthatswana—comprised six non-contiguous regions. Its infrastructure, roads and transport system were poorly developed and it suffered the political and socio-economic disadvantages of being a marginalised 'bantustan' of the South African government. Yet, the people (and educators in particular) were able to 'pick themselves up off the dust' and tackle the challenges of under-resourced schools, overcrowded classes, demoralised communities and poorly qualified teachers. The result was in many respects remarkable. Hartshorne (1992) acknowledged that the PEUP had transformed classrooms and was an important primary school initiative in Africa.

## The Process Exemplified

Let us return to Mafikeng to see the classroom upgrading process played out, but this time in a school situated in a traditional village on the southern side of town. Again, given its close proximity to town, this school was over-subscribed. The high pupil enrolment had compelled teachers to work in cramped conditions in various outbuildings and in a nearby church.

When I first visited the church, it contained 150 3rd-grade children: three classes each of 50 learners, situated in different sections of the church (nave and transepts). In such a context, there were certainly inconveniences but none proving insurmountable to the job of teaching. Portable blackboards were used and were stacked away at the back of the building at the end of each day. Kneeling at the pews, children used the seating in front for writing surfaces. A home-made trolley library was sometimes used to take books from one classroom to another for the daily reading periods.

During the next few years, the children of this school raised funds that were used to build and equip additional classrooms. They did so by collecting and selling empty cool-drink bottles and tins for recycling purposes. I recall arriving at the school one day to find a huge pile of bones that was about to be collected and paid for by a local fertilizer company. Thus, the children were able to move from over-crowded outbuildings into comfortable classroom environments with their own desks and chairs.

## Lessons in the Field

By 1996, the recommended polices and practices of the PEUP had, to a large extent, become integrated into the educational system of the North West Province. What might be learnt from some of the PEUP-related field experiences described in this chapter? One important insight is that much can be achieved from the small beginnings of "ordinary" teachers. Old tomato boxes were used for shelving where there were insufficient funds to buy wooden shelving; empty card-board boxes were used to build shops in the corner of classrooms where junior primary children could role-play and practise their mathematics in counting change; old magazines and newspapers were used in creative ways to enrich and stimulate language; stones, bottle tops and sucker sticks were used for counting purposes. Within this environment, we soon saw how readily and competently teachers were able to manage classes of 50 learners.

An invaluable support for teachers of large classes is the avail-ability of suitable learning materials. It was our experience, however, that such materials were put to far better use if the teachers had participated in their production. Thus simple workshops for teachers are strongly recommended. In addition to producing usable materi-als, the exercise itself (of designing and creating materials) provides a most effective means of in-service training for teachers of large classes. The 1st-grade teachers in the PEUP who "rolled up their sleeves", painted their classrooms and began displaying children's work on the walls, made visible to other teachers and to the local community that they were serious about making improvements in their classes. This set in motion a sense of commitment that soon

*An invaluable support for teachers of large classes is the availability of suitable learning materials. It was our experience, however, that such materials were put to far better use if the teachers had parti-cipated in their production.*

proved infectious and gathered momentum. In due course, these teachers demonstrated how, by being prepared beforehand, they were able to educate most effectively classes of 50 learners.

I believe that a key ingredient for the PEUP was that teachers worked together, supporting each other in coping with large classes. Exemplary teaching practices were developed which served to inspire teachers from adjacent classrooms and neighbouring schools. Ideally this should be facilitated and supported by the Department of Education or at least the local education office. However, as such support is so often not forthcoming in developing contexts, schools may need to take the initiative themselves, preferably in partnership with a teacher-education institution and sponsor, and with at least the blessing and knowledge of the Department of Education.

The local school communities were informed of developments and involved in the process. Indeed, it was the participation of parents and other community members in the PEUP that made it possible for teachers to provide quality learning experiences in their large classes. Recall, for example, how adults in the community assisted by making bookshelves and teaching apparatus and, if literate, by listening to young children read when the teacher was busy teaching groups.

Finally, landmarks and achievements along the way need to be celebrated by the teachers. PEUP and regional conventions proved to be particularly effective for the professional development of teachers and in building a strong sense of mutual support and commitment to the task of educational improvement.

## Teacher Education

Teacher education institutions have an important role to play in meeting the challenges of large-class teaching. They can research educational needs and identify and analyse good practices in local schools. Through their lecture programmes, they can promote a fuller understanding of contextual factors that influence how teachers teach; they can make student teachers aware of the wide range of teaching and assessment strategies that can be used in large classes. As far as is appropriate and possible, they should practise such strategies themselves when lecturing to large classes of education students.

In higher degree programmes, and in short courses for senior education personnel, tertiary institutions should promote a systemic understanding of school improvement. As demonstrated in the PEUP large classes, in order to improve the classroom learning environment and quality of teaching, a holistic, whole-school development approach needs to be adopted. Principals and government officials need to recognise the vital role they and the local school communities play in supporting teachers of large classes.

Teacher education institutions can often go further by supporting project initiatives and planned interventions to develop effective schools as centres of excellence and to facilitate the production of learning materials by teachers for large-class contexts.

## Concluding Thoughts

The rich field experiences we gained over the 16-year life of the Primary Education Upgrading Programme showed us how remarkably creative and resourceful teachers can be in addressing such problems as overcrowding despite the odds being heavily stacked against them. We came to realize how important it is for teachers of large classes to be actively supported by the school principal and to be stimulated by periodic visits to neighbouring schools and simple workshops with teachers in similar circumstances. We saw how professionally empowering it is when teachers mutually reinforce each other over a period of time. We saw how effectively teachers could transform their drab and dreary classrooms into stimulating places of learning and convert waste materials into useful learning aids.

As our experience demonstrated, such teams of local 'ordinary' teachers—teachers who daily work at the chalk face of large classes—can transform the quality of large-class teaching in a region. In due course, they can be promoted beyond their classrooms to become champions of a large-scale teaching and learning reform project. While it is probable that whole-class, expository teaching will be the most frequently used strategy, a recent workshop I conducted with teachers of large classes in the Nelson Mandela Metropole identified that many more strategies can be used (Holderness, 2000).

It is my firm belief that meetings of concerned practitioners can provide the impetus for shared reform initiatives and mutual support. At such meetings, achievable goals should be identified, inspirational talks be given and, most of all, visits should be made to classes where progress is being made in coping with large classes. From such gatherings can emerge local teams of 'leading teachers' who can continue to inspire, encourage and guide fellow teachers in the district.

# References

Hartshone, K. (1992). *Crisis and challenge: Black education 1910 – 1990*. Oxford, UK: Oxford University Press.

Holderness, W. (1986). *Upgrading primary education in the seventeen circuits*. Occasional Publication. South Africa: University of Bophuthatswana.

Holderness, W. (1992). *Grade 1 teacher's handbook. A cross-curricular guide*. Pretoria, South Africa: Colibri Publishers.

Holderness, W. (1993). *Grade 2 teacher's handbook*: Pretoria, South Africa: Colibri Publishers.

Holderness, W. (2000) *Teaching, learning and assessment strategies*. P102 Study Guide. South Africa: University of Port Elizabeth.

Holderness, W. (2001). HIV/AIDS and education: Implications and responses. ILISO 'The Eye', 5 (1), 24-34. *Journal of the Institute for Social and Systemic Change*. South Africa: University of Port Elizabeth.

UNESCO. (1998). *World education report 1998*. Paris: UNESCO.

UNICEF. (1998). *The state of the world's children*. New York: UNICEF.

Watkins, K. (2000). *The Oxfam education report*. Oxford, UK: Oxfam.

# About the Author

**Bill Holderness**, Ph D, is a Professor of Education at the University of Port Elizabeth, South Africa. He grew up in Zimbabwe, studied in South Africa and completed his Master's and Doctoral degrees at the University of London. His 30 years of teaching in South Africa have been in a variety of institutions, including schools, a college of education, and two universities. Over the years, Bill Holderness has initiated, coordinated and evaluated a number of large-scale, school improvement projects, particularly in the rural and marginalised areas of South Africa. He has also had extensive field experience in conducting in-service teacher education workshops in disadvantaged schools where large classes and limited resources are the norm. E-mail: ttawlh@upe.ac.za

# CHAPTER 2

# Teaching Large Classes in China

*Cheng Yuanshan & Rosalind Y. Mau*

Today in China, most of the primary and high school teachers teach large classes. This situation has been the norm for several decades. However, recently in some large Chinese cities, an experiment on teaching small classes is being conducted to meet the requirements of Quality Driven Education proposed by the Chinese Education Ministry. In the world, most teachers prefer teaching small classes (Din, 1998; Sarason, 1990; Harap, 1959). If it is not possible to teach small classes, what can teachers do to reach instructional objectives? What strategies can we learn from Chinese teachers who teach large classes?

## Class Size in China

In China, all children are required to attend school for 9 years. This compulsory education usually consists of 6 years in primary school and 3 years in junior high school. After that, a 3-year senior high school education is required if students want to enter a university. Schools have a fixed number of students in a class. A group of students assigned to a class will remain in the same classroom to learn different subjects. Similarly, university undergraduate students are assigned to classes which function in the same way.

The National Education Association of America (1965) defined a class as the number of students a teacher is responsible for in a self-contained classroom. Ross and McKenna (1955) defined a class as any group of students scheduled to meet regularly in a school day with a teacher to learn some specific part of the school's curriculum. Different researchers define "large class" and "small class" differently. That makes it difficult to interpret and discuss research results. Some researchers define "small classes" as anything under 40 students and "large classes" as having over 50 students. Other researchers define "small classes" as having less than 15 students and "large classes" as more than 25. According to Ross and McKenna (1955), the Metropolitan School Study Council of America set 20 to 25 as the upper limit of small classes and 30 to 35 as the lower limit of large classes.

Usually, in statistical data, class size is not listed as an index; instead, the student-teacher ratio is provided. In the year 2000, there were around 582,300 primary schools with about 135,479,600 primary students and 64,400 junior high schools with about 21,834,400 students in China (http://www.edu.cn). In various areas of China, education is developed differently. There are more schools in large cities than in remote districts. In the rural areas, large classes are the result of numerous students and insufficient teachers. Many of these classes are even multi-aged, where a teacher teaches students of various ages. Much of the available data do not provide accurate information for different areas and, therefore, this chapter focuses on data from Beijing only.

Compared to other cities or rural districts and as the capital and education centre, Beijing has a high quality of education. For example, Beijing has over 50 universities, the most in the world. In the year of 2000, there were 2,169 primary schools with 743,109 students and a total of 58,002 full-time primary school teachers. Thus, for primary school, the student-teacher ratio was 12.81:1. There were 512,351 junior high school students and 36,030 full-time teachers. The student-teacher ratio was 14.22:1. For senior high schools, there were 179,002 students and 12,873 full-time teachers. The student-teacher ratio was 13.91:1 ( http://www.bjedu.gov.cn/zlzx/sytj/). The statistical data are interesting since the student-teacher ratio is low for both primary school and high school. The ratio is lower than that reported in the United States in the 1970s. For example, in 1975 in the United States, at the primary level, the student-teacher ratio was 21.7:1 and at the high school level it was 18.8:1 (U.S. National Center for Education Statistics, 1976). Another interesting point is that, in Beijing, the ratio for primary school was lower than that for high school. One of the possible reasons is that the one-child-per-family policy of birth control was successfully implemented and resulted in the enrollment in primary schools decreasing in the last few years. For example, in the year 2000, in Beijing, there were 185,059 students who graduated from primary schools compared to 92,002 students who enrolled as primary-one students (http://www.bjedu.gov.cn/zlzx/sytj/).

Although the student-teacher ratios were low in Beijing, most classes are large in the rest of China. Usually, in cities—including Beijing—a class has about 40 students. Din (1998) surveyed Chinese rural schoolteachers on class size. Responses from 55 teachers with more than 5 years of teaching experience indicated that they taught larger classes of 50 students. Why is the student-teacher ratio not high in Beijing despite the large classes? One of the reasons is that in high schools, each teacher teaches only one subject. Even in primary schools most teachers teach only one subject. For example, in Beijing, only 15,887 of 58,002 full-time primary school teachers teach both mathematics and Chinese language (http://www.bjedu.gov.cn/zlzx/sytj/). The rest of the full-time teachers teach only one of the following subjects: moral education, Chinese language, mathematics, foreign language, sciences, geography, history, physical education, music, arts or computer education.

Another possible reason is that the Ministry of Education in China suggests upper teaching limits for the teachers. For example, it is suggested that no more than 15 periods of teaching should be assigned to every junior high school teacher and no more than 12 periods to every senior high school teacher per week.

## Traditional Teaching in China

Back in olden times, large classes were not the norm in China. In fact, much of the teaching was conducted on a one-to-one basis. Rich families hired teachers to teach their own children at home. Later on, some villages had old-style private schools where one teacher taught some students of the village. The class size was small and all students of different ages sat in the same classroom. The modern schools and public schools were set up in the late 1800s and early 1900s. At that time, teaching large classes started because more children entered the school system.

*In their learning process, usually Chinese students are highly motivated and have the ability to self-regulate their own classroom behaviors. There are hardly any severe discipline problems in classrooms and most students concentrate on what a teacher is saying.*

No matter the size of classes, mainstream education in China is achievement-driven or, more accurately stated, examination-driven. For over 1,000 years, the most important educational goal for students and teachers was to achieve good results in examinations. In ancient China, the government officers were selected by nationwide examinations. The only way to have a respected career was to learn diligently and to pass the national examination successfully. Today, since not all students with qualified knowledge and abilities get into universities, the national university entrance examination functions as a selection device for admission. To enter a high school with a high-achieving reputation, students also take entrance examinations. These examinations are achievement assessments; they are highly related to the content knowledge of different subjects. Almost all are closed-book examinations and almost no performance examinations are used.

In this kind of educational environment, except for moral education, the Chinese education system emphasizes knowledge and skill transfer in the cognitive domain. Although the instructional objectives are related to all the six levels of the cognitive domain listed in Blooms Taxonomy (Bloom, 1956), creativity and other abilities in the affective domain are not given much attention.

*To teach large classes and to engage students, the key solution for Chinese teachers is to prepare their lessons well. Teachers use direct instruction which is a very effective and powerful way to reach the learning objectives of high achievement.*

Following tradition, teacher-directed teaching is used in most Chinese classrooms. Generally, teachers or professors only bring a textbook to the classroom and during the lessons they talk almost all the time. The only "teaching tool" for most teachers is a piece of chalk. However, for reaching the goal of good examination scores, the Chinese education system is rather successful and Chinese students have shown admirable achievements in the world. For example, every year in worldwide mathematics and science competitions, Chinese students achieve high results.

## Achievement and Teaching Strategies

Studies have shown contradictory results on the relationship between class size and achievements (Educational Research Service, 1978; Glass, Cahen, Smith, & Filby, 1982; Spitzer, 1954). Some studies reported that small classes were better, while some studies showed large classes were better, and yet others found no difference.

Studies on the relationship between class size and achievement involve many variables. For example, as research subjects, students' ages, genders, grade levels, ability levels and socio-economic backgrounds may influence academic results. Content matter or the subjects of learning vary in difficulty and may influence students' achievement. The ability, experience, education, or attitude of teachers may also influence the relationship between class size and achievement. For instance, the results of a study by Johnson (1977) suggest that the students performed better not only because they were in small classes but also because their teachers were trained better. Likewise, results of a study by Cahen, Filby, McCutcheon and Kyle (1983) indicate that besides class size, teachers' beliefs, attitude, knowledge and skills influenced their instruction and students' performance.

Since teacher-related factors perform important roles in students' achievement and Chinese students generally perform well in achievement assessment, we need to find out what Chinese teachers do in their classes and how they prepare their lessons.

In their learning process, usually Chinese students are highly motivated and have the ability to self-regulate their own classroom behaviors. There are hardly any severe discipline problems in classrooms and most students concentrate on what a teacher is saying. However, teaching large classes is clearly a challenge. Two major problems that arise in China are how to manage large classes and

*Collaboration among teachers is very much encouraged. Some schools urge teachers to prepare their lessons together and to help each other in dealing with teaching difficulties. In delivering a well-planned lesson, teachers define and elaborate the concepts clearly. While teaching the concepts, they carefully select and provide different examples.*

how to customize teaching to different ability levels of students in these classes. In large classes, the communication between teachers and students may be a challenge because it is difficult for teachers to observe and assess all students' responses. Thus, it may seem impossible for teachers to take care of all students with different ability levels and adjust teaching plans quickly.

To teach large classes and to engage students, the key solution for Chinese teachers is to prepare their lessons well. Teachers use direct instruction, which is a very effective and powerful way to reach the learning objectives of high achievement. In direct instruction, less student activities decrease the possibility of management difficulties in the classroom. Usually, most of the teachers in China are well grounded in the subject knowledge and skills they teach. The Ministry of Education limits the teaching hours of teachers and provides more time for them to prepare their lessons. According to the requirement of the Chinese Ministry of Education, the time ratio of preparation to teaching is 5:1. As previously stated, high school teachers and a large portion of primary school teachers teach one subject. Although they may teach different classes, these classes are usually in the same grade. So they prepare fewer but better lessons.

Collaboration among teachers is very much encouraged. Some schools urge teachers to prepare their lessons together and to help each other in dealing with teaching difficulties. Various and novel ways of delivering lessons are promoted in schools. In delivering a well-planned lesson, teachers define and elaborate the concepts clearly. While teaching the concepts, they carefully select and provide different examples. Thus, students are engaged in learning the subject matter and grasp the concepts successfully. Of course when students feel they are learning something and enjoy the lessons, there are less discipline problems or classroom management problems.

Lam, Ma & Wong (1999) investigated how mathematics teachers adapted the national curriculum to large classes. They used ethnographic

*Oftentimes, teachers knew each student in their classes and were able to call the students by name. So teachers were able to personalize their teaching and develop a spirit of community even in these large classes.*

methods such as interviews and observations over 4 weeks in a rural and an urban elementary school. In both schools, the teachers followed the requirements of the textbooks. They had a strong influence on how the subject was planned and delivered. Their decisions were based on professional knowledge, their educational beliefs and the public examination. Teachers used the blackboard to write key words, concepts, numbers and whatever was important and appropriate for the lesson. Lessons were organized and clearly articulated to the students. Oftentimes, teachers knew each student in their classes and were able to call the students by name. So teachers were able to personalize their teaching and develop a spirit of community even in these large classes.

## Teacher Training in China

Teacher training is an important factor in preparing teachers to teach large classes in China. For primary school teachers, upon graduation from junior high school, they are required to finish a 4-year program in teachers' training schools. In the training schools, they learn basic subjects which they will teach in the future and pedagogy subjects. They also attend teaching practices in primary schools. For high school teachers, the basic requirement is that after finishing senior high school, they study for 4 years in normal universities and graduate with a high school teaching qualification. During their study in normal universities, they learn the subject which they will teach as their major course of study and do teaching practice during their last year.

*During the teaching practicum, training teachers must first prepare their lessons and present them to their classmates and their supervisors. After receiving suggestions and criticisms on the lesson, they are required to modify and correct any mistakes they made. Then they will teach in front of their peers and supervisors again. When their lessons meet all the criteria of a good practicum, they will deliver the lessons to children in the schools.*

During the program, the training teachers go to schools and observe many different lessons delivered by master teachers. Through observations, they learn how master teachers organize their lessons and engage students. They also take notes on all details of the lesson development. After the observation, a reflection lesson is usually conducted. At this time, master teachers explain the reasons for conducting the lesson in certain ways and share their teaching experiences. When the training teachers return to the universities or teacher training schools, they have further discussions on the lesson under the guidance of supervisors or professors. The training teachers are asked to summarize the strengths and weaknesses of the observed lessons. Moreover, they are required to point out what they have learned and how they will teach in the future when they have their own classes.

During the teaching practicum, prior to teaching in classes, training teachers must prepare their lessons and present them to their classmates and their supervisors. After receiving suggestions and criticisms on the lesson, they are required to modify and correct any mistakes they made. Then they will teach in front of their peers and supervisors again. When their lessons meet all the criteria of a good practicum they will deliver the lessons to children in the schools.

Thus, most teachers generally are well grounded in the subject area that they teach because they have studied the basics and enrolled in advanced courses in their field. In addition, they have time to translate their basic knowledge into worthwhile lessons for large classes and have practiced teaching before entering schools.

## The Quality Driven Education Initiative

Although large classes are the norm in China and many students have high achievements, some weaknesses related to large-class teaching have surfaced. In the new millennium, China faces the challenge of a global economy. For the education system, it is not enough to train students only for achieving high scores in examinations. Increasingly, teachers are required to teach students with different abilities and to focus on more creativity in their classes. In response to this global challenge, the Chinese Ministry of Education proposed the initiative of Quality Driven Education, in which priority is given to develop the students' creativity and different abilities.

However, in China, the instructional methods in large classes are still quite uniform. In classrooms, students spend most of their time listening to the teachers' instruction, taking notes and doing written exercises. Students are seldom exposed to performance tasks and group activities. In a study of secondary school teachers, Zhang (1997) examined the difficulties in implementing a communicative approach to language instruction. A salient difficulty was the pressure of external examinations on both teachers and students. Briefly, a communicative approach is more student-orientated and considers students' needs and interests. Active modes of learning include group work and improvised practice, developing more flexible minds and inspiring confidence in coping with unanticipated situations. Moreover, teaching is not restricted to the textbook and teachers use their professional expertise to teach more flexibly.

Based on a survey, Din (1998) reported that school teachers in China thought that smaller classes were easier to manage, more effective, provided for individualized help to students, and required less work. They also felt that competitive class activities would improve their students' academic achievement. Teachers felt that, in small classes, they would know more about their students and be able to use different instructional methods to meet the needs of different students.

In the year 2000, an experimental study on small-class teaching was initiated in several Chinese large cities, including Shanghai, Beijing and Tianjin. More than 300 primary schools in Shanghai started to have small classes of around 25 students. Each class had two classrooms in which an IT learning corner, toy corner, science corner and exhibition corner were included. It was reported that the students enjoyed the new ways of learning and developed their different abilities. In Beijing, about 1,000 small classes were set up to study teaching of small classes.

Regardless of the findings of such studies, the challenges of adequate resources—especially qualified teachers—remain. As a consequence, China and many other countries will continue to have large classes. The Quality Driven Education Initiative in China would stand to gain from research on large-class teaching as well.

## Conclusion

Large classes are predominant in all levels of schools in China today. Although it is difficult to use a variety of instructional methods in large classes, teachers manage to help their students achieve academically. Teachers both in primary and high schools usually follow a textbook-centered approach to teach a national curriculum. In China, large classes appear as effective as small classes because educational goals involve learning factual information and comprehending that information.

Our observations of large-class teaching in China point to the importance of teachers' attitudes, knowledge and skills. In China, sound teacher training is clearly a priority. Trainee teachers observe master teachers, reflect upon lessons and practice teaching before they begin to teach children. Qualified teachers are expected to be well grounded in the subject(s) they teach. They are given adequate time to prepare their lessons and to collaborate with other teachers. In these ways, teachers in China are well prepared to handle large classes and teach the subject area well.

# References

Bloom, B. S.(Ed.). (1956). *Taxonomy of educational objectives: Handbook I. Cognitive Domain.* New York: D. McKay.

Cahen, L., Filby, N., McCutcheon, G., & Kyle, D. (1983). *Class size and instruction.* New York: Longman.

Din, F. S. (1998, October). *The functions of class size perceived by Chinese rural school teachers.* Paper presented at the Research Forum of the National Rural Education Association, Buffalo, New York.

Educational Research Service (1978), *Class size: A summary of research.* Virginia: Educational Research Service, Inc.

Glass, G. V., Cahen, L. S., Smith, M. L., & Filby, N. N. (1982). *School class size—research and policy.* Beverly Hills, CA: Sage Publications.

Harap, H. (1959). Many factors affect teacher morale. *Nation's Schools, 63 (June),* 55-57.

Johnson L. M. (1977). South Carolina first grade pilot project 1975-76: The effects of class size on reading and mathematics achievement. *Office of Research Report Series* (Vol. 1).

Lam, C., Ma, Y., & Wong, N. (1999, April). *Teacher development, not accountability control, is the key to successful curriculum implementation: A case study of two primary schools in Northeast China.* Paper presented at the Annual Meeting of the American Educational Research Association, Montreal, Canada.

National Education Association of America (1965). Class size in kindergarten and elementary schools. *Research Report (March 1965, p. 27).*

Ross, D. H. & Mckenna, B. (1955). *Class size: The multi-million dollar question.* New York: Institute of Administration Research, Teachers College, Columbia University.

Sarason, S. (1990). *The predictable failure of educational reform.* San Francisco: Jossey-Bass.

Spitzer, F. B. (1954). Class size and student achievement in elementary schools. *Elementary School Journal*, 55, 82-86.

U.S. National Center for Education Statistics (1976). *Statistics of public elementary and secondary day schools.* Washington, D.C.: U.S. Government Printing Office.

Zhang, M. (1997). *The difficulties and challenges of adopting the communicative approach in TEFL at secondary school in Qinghai Province, China.* ERIC ED413790.

http://www.bjedu.gov.cn/zlzx/sytj/ (accessed on 14 October 2001)

http://www.edu.cn (accessed on 14 October 2001)

# About the Authors

**Cheng Yuanshan,** Ph D, is an assistant professor in the Psychological Studies Academic Group, National Institute of Education, Nanyang Technological University, Singapore. He obtained his Bachelor and Master degrees at Beijing Normal University, and taught in China for years. He also taught at the University of Ottawa, Canada. As a cognitive psychologist, his current work focuses on human judgments and decision-making. In the education area, he works on discipline problems and gender differences in Singapore schools. E-mail: yscheng@nie. edu.sg

**Rosalind Y. Mau,** Ph D, was an associate professor in the Policy and Management Academic Group, National Institute of Education, Nanyang Technological University, Singapore. She worked with Cheng Yuanshan on a study of resilience of secondary school students in large classes in Singapore. E-mail: rosalindmau@hotmail.com

# CHAPTER 3

# The 'Art' of Teaching Large Classes in India

*Pradnya Patet & Meera Oke*

Educational psychologists have continuously reiterated the fact that teaching is an art and a science (Samaras, 2000; Woolfolk, 1998). Scientifically, we rely upon a research-based body of knowledge that defines the psychological, socio-emotional and cultural influences on the process of teaching and learning. The 'art' of teaching, however, develops from a hands-on experience of applying the scientific knowledge in individual cultural contexts, recognizing the impact of individual personality characteristics and reflecting on practice. The process is very similar to the way in which an artist explores, mixes and matches a variety of scientific techniques of painting to create a masterpiece that reflects individuality and the cultural influence.

This conceptualization becomes slightly perplexing—or even overwhelming—when we consider the large class size in India. When most of the current research is geared towards reducing the class size to ensure quality learning and teaching and higher level thinking (Bredekamp & Copple, 1997; Mosteller, 1995), does teaching in large classrooms have anything to contribute to our continual quest to understand the complex process of teaching and learning? We believe it does. In this chapter, we would like to take you into some of the classrooms in Mumbai, India, and introduce you to the 'art' of teaching large classes in an effective manner.

Current constructivist philosophy has redefined the role of students and teachers as that of active constructors of knowledge who seek to make sense of their worlds by making direct connections from their experiences (Bredekamp & Copple, 1997; Bredekamp & Rosegrant, 1995). Is it possible for a large class to reflect, through its practice, a theoretical framework such as constructivism? Can this large class size emphasize a close relationship between the teacher and individual students? We find that teachers in large classes take on the same roles as their colleagues in small classes, but implement specific methods and techniques in a manner appropriate to the class size that they are dealing with. Our aim is to document the 'art' of teaching large classes as it is experienced in the Indian context and dispel the myth that in all large classes students learn by passively listening to the teacher who transmits his/her knowledge through large chunks of direct instruction.

## Getting Ready to Paint

Before painting a masterpiece, an artist gets ready by exploring and understanding the nature of the available materials. The intended backdrop, paper or canvas, the possible color schemes and the various tools for painting are considerations that help an artist plan. Similarly, getting ready to plunge into the 'art' of teaching requires that we explore and understand our existing cultural patterns and beliefs and the existing set up of the educational institutions within a societal context. The cultural patterns and values explain some natural techniques that sink into effective practice. So, before we get into the actual painting techniques involved in the 'art' of teaching large classes, let us explore and understand the canvas, color scheme and painting tools that we have to work with.

*Cultural Patterns, Attitudes and Beliefs*   Sub-cultural diversity that includes a variety of religions, customs, traditions, lifestyles, 16 national languages and innumerable dialects makes it impossible to speak of India in generic terms. However, there are some universal cultural attitudes towards education that govern the way in which teachers connect with their students. This involves socialization goals, the involvement of parents in their child's work at school, the way in which discipline is executed in the classroom and the need to teach children to incorporate it into their lives as a tool for healthy physical and mental living.

Traditionally, the Indian culture incorporates a sense of reverence for the teaching profession, besides a basic respect for experienced individuals (Bajpayee, 1988). The belief that with age comes experience and wisdom dictates a respectful attitude in behavior towards teachers (Saraswathi & Dutta, 1988). Families emphasize respect for a teacher's authority. The overall reverence that is observed towards any elder in the community extends to the student-teacher relationship and, therefore, the student-teacher relationship is akin to that of a parent and child (Shantiniketan, 1954). Later in this chapter, we write about emotional bonding as a means to motivate both the teacher and the learner. At this point in the chapter, suffice to say that teacher authority is a dominant absolute force in creating and maintaining an atmosphere of responsible and concentrated learning. The nature of such authority and position communicates the unspoken cultural premise that the teacher and student share the responsibility of learning (Bajpayee, 1988).

The respect for such authority binds parents and teachers together and strengthens the development of children. Parents range from those who are illiterate to highly educated professionals. Although clashes in philosophies about teaching and learning exist, the teacher's views carry more weight and disagreements are sorted out between the adults. The lesson for children is universal: respect an adult's views and recognize the advantages or good intentions behind the actions (Narain, 1964).

We see evidence of this respect for authority in the response that children give teachers when disciplined or when subjected to general 'words of wisdom' from a teacher's personal experience. It is not unusual for teachers in India to talk about life beyond the classroom during a lesson. Students will never 'talk back' to a teacher and will consider suggestions provided by the teacher with no overt resistance whether or not they choose to follow through with them. Often, the 'teacher authority' described here may be interpreted by western worlds as 'unquestionable passive obedience', or a 'fearful respect' that stimulates and sustains heteronomy, where heteronomy is 'doing something' simply because someone tells you to in order to avoid punishment and/or be rewarded (Piaget, 1965). Our experience as participants in the Indian culture, though, is different.

The authority and reverence attributed to the teaching profession, irrespective of the individual person in that role, is one of awe and earned respect. Challenge and questioning are valued to the extent that they are expressed in a culturally appropriate manner, recognizing and respecting the age and experience of the person being addressed. If the child disagrees about an event, he/she brings the evidence to the class with the teacher's permission (due respect to the teacher). In essence, this cultural value translates itself into a universal value that teaches individuals to think internally about content, feelings and the influence of their actions on others before engaging in an act, even though it may pertain to a neutral intellectual fact. Thus, this cultural basis of the teacher-student relationship lays down the foundation for autonomous thinking where autonomy is 'doing something' after a careful consideration of all possible relevant factors and how the final decision will affect others around you (Piaget, 1965).

In India, education is considered the best way to be successful in life. In most middle class urban communities—and increasingly now, in the rural areas—children's roles are defined in terms of school. Thus, education comes first and adults urge children to focus on their studies while parents provide the basic needs until the education is complete. Children in middle class homes normally do not move out and support themselves while they are completing their education. Rituals, traditions and customs reflect a reverence for education. In some communities, the wedding ceremony includes a ritual during which the bride seeks the blessings of and pays tribute to her first teacher. During a special festival, 'Saraswati puja' or "pati (the slate/book) puja" that celebrates knowledge, books are placed at the altar. The teacher is never addressed by his/her first name but with titles like 'Sir' and 'Ma'am' even after the teacher retires. The ultimate reverence for a teacher is echoed in the 'shloka' (a hymn from the Hindu religious texts):

> "Gurur Brahma, Gurur Vishnu, Gurur devo Maheshwara.
> Gurur Saakshat par Brahma, Tasmayee shree Gurvenamaha"

The hymn is one of adoration for the Guru (teacher) whose role is equated to that of Brahma (creator), Vishnu (sustainer), and Maheshwara (destroyer) the three main Gods in the Hindu faith and mythology.

***The Existing Set Up***    Children in India usually begin kindergarten at age 3 and 1st grade at age 5. After 10th grade, they do 2 years of junior college and then, may pursue a Bachelor's degree for 3 to 5 years depending on the field. Most children in urban areas complete their school years and several move on to junior college. Primary education is free for all children attending 'municipal schools'. The municipal schools often draw populations from the lower socio-economic group, the government-aided (partially funded) schools bring in the middle class and the private schools invite the upper-middle and upper classes.

Our chapter focuses on the 'middle class schools' where parents and teachers strive to help children succeed in school in the hope that they will be able to climb up the socioeconomic ladder. Most children in these schools continue with college studies and tend to have focused goals and high aspirations. Teachers, too, come from similar backgrounds and have similar values. These common goals bind the schools together although the actual techniques, methods and styles vary from school to school and even class to class. In our attempt to communicate the 'art' of effective teaching in large classrooms, we have selected examples from a variety of classrooms in Mumbai, a large metropolitan city in which many sub-cultures co-exist.

*A Typical School Day* 9:25 a.m.! The bell rings. Some 'early birds' scramble to their classrooms from the playground where they have been playing. Other children are already in their rooms before the bell rings. Students settle down at assigned desks. The teacher enters. Hushed verbal messaging sweeps through the class followed by silence. The students rise and greet the teacher. The teacher records attendance. He or she then escorts the class to 'school assembly' where all classes gather for some form of reflective meditation led by the principal.

Each class returns to its classroom and follows a set timetable given at the beginning of the year. The academic routine includes timed instruction for a range of curricular subjects, including art, music, physical education, sewing, and depending on the age, some cultural arts and crafts like batik-making, folk dance, drama and horticulture. Different teachers come in to teach different subjects for periods of 35 minutes each. Some subjects may be allocated double periods (that is, of 70 minutes at a stretch). The bell rings at the end of each period. Children stay on in one classroom as teachers move in and out. Children attend 7 to 8 periods in a day with two short recesses and a lunch break.

During the recesses, children run to the playground, chat with their friends or play sedentary games in the room. Noise levels

*Those unfamiliar with these large crowd transitions may react with questions about the children's safety and the school's sense of accountability. Insiders consider these questions hypothetical and instead, may be more able than the outsider to recognize the potential for the children in this crowd to develop interdependence, responsibility and even a field independent cognitive style.*

during this time are high and considered appropriate. For the lunch break, the teacher escorts the children to a cafeteria or a huge hall and leaves, while the teacher on duty oversees all assembled there. After eating, children engage in spontaneous, self-organized play in little groups. At the end of this 45-minute break, each class lines up and returns to the classroom. Class monitors, selected by teachers or elected by classmates at the beginning of the year, help maintain the order during this time.

School ends at approximately 4:00 p.m. School-bus children leave first and then the rest. Children find their way to their parents, guardians, servants or whoever is taking them home. They often help each other to get through the swarming crowd to the right place. Older siblings find their younger ones and take responsibility for escorting them. Those unfamiliar with these large crowd transitions may react with questions about the children's safety and the school's sense of accountability. Insiders consider these questions hypothetical and instead, may be more able than the outsider to recognize the potential for the children in this crowd to develop interdependence, responsibility and even a field independent cognitive style.

Other signs of structured discipline exist in the overall classroom culture: school uniforms; notebooks covered with brown paper; behaviors like standing up when answering or asking a question. Where, in this traditional set up, is there scope for constructivist learning and teaching to take place? The answer to this question lies in the techniques and methods that teachers use within the existing structure.

## The Painting Begins

*Sponge Painting and the Instructor Role*   The teacher playing the 'instructor' role provides students with concrete blocks of information much like a sponge that makes bold imprints on paper. The outcome ultimately depends on each student's previous background and intellectual level. In a large class, the teacher's success in playing the instructor role depends on how well the teacher can hold the attention of the large group by making the information relevant to each individual. Consider the following scenario.

In a 4th-grade classroom, the teacher was teaching about time differences. She narrated a story about Jaya who was eager to celebrate her 6th birthday. Jaya was expecting all her friends and was very excited at the thought of the party games, the special kheer (sweet) her mother would make, her new dress and of course, the presents. There was one thing though that made Jaya a little sad. Bapu, her father, wasn't going to be there. He was away in America. He had promised her that he would call to wish her a happy birthday. As the day went by, Jaya kept wondering if he would forget to call. The party was finally over. Jaya, tired from all the excitement, was ready to fall asleep. Just then the phone rang and sure enough it was Bapu. Jaya asked, "But why didn't you call earlier? It's nearly over now." "No, it isn't," said her father, "In fact, it's just beginning here in America. Wait till I get back and I will explain."

The teacher told the class how Jaya's father used a globe, when he returned, to explain how the earth turned around its own axis, while it also circled the sun and how that made night and day. At this point, the teacher herself held up a globe, moving it as Jaya's father might have in the story. The children learned geography, science, social studies and language in an integrated manner. The story about Jaya made the learning relevant and enjoyable because a birthday disappointment was something that all the children could identify with. The teacher then went on to explain, still using the globe, the hemispheres, and the latitudes and longitudes. Since the example came before she defined concepts related to the topic of time differences, the children were able to grasp these concepts and their abstract definitions easily. Stigler & Stevenson (1991) reiterate the importance of elaborating on concrete, real life problems and situations before providing abstract, conceptual definitions.

***Brush Painting and the Validator Role*** Brush strokes often smooth the paint on the picture or polish it to make it shine. So does the teacher when he/she validates and acknowledges the knowledge acquired by the class through a series of assignments, projects and healthy competition. It is important to validate children's play and learning so that they may be ready for new information (Bredekamp & Copple, 1997; Berk & Winsler, 1995; Muralidharan & Pankajam, 1988). The goal is to help students maintain a state of equilibrium before reactivating the schemes through a cognitive conflict. In large classes, since individualized validation is hard, validation takes place through a wide variety of projects and assignments. The following project in a 3rd-grade classroom highlights how validation takes place at the student's individual pace and incorporates a wide variety of skills in a comprehensive context rather than an isolated skill that has just been taught.

The 3rd-grade class was studying profit and loss. The topic, introduced through direct instruction, included relevant examples of how the isolated problems in the text related to real life. Students were then asked to bring in one item from home to sell. The item had to have a price tag and the owner needed to know what the original price was and decide how much of a profit she was going to make. Most classes comprise of four groups sometimes called 'houses'. This arrangement makes competitions, group projects, and other assignments that require group work convenient. Each 'house' had 3 days to display their items and 'sell' their merchandise. The total cost of merchandise left over was to be deducted from the team's total. Each individual in the class had a certain allocated amount of money to spend. During math class, while others were working on paper and pencil problems related to the topic, each house left their seats for 10 minutes at a time to scrutinize the merchandise and decide what they could afford. They could, during recess, bargain with the owner to see if the price could be lowered. The shopping time lasted for a total of 15 days. At the end of this display, each house had to figure out how much profit they made and which items incurred a loss. They also had to determine whether the items that incurred a loss were substantiated through the profit made by other items.

The activity validated several basic skills such as addition and subtraction, recognizing that those were crucial in order to understand the concept of profit and loss. Children had the opportunity to take their own time to calculate their expenses and decide how they wanted to spend their money. They had the opportunity to help each other with their calculations. In addition to all these experiences, it is important to realize that the opportunity to leave their desks and experience the same topic in a hands-on manner enhances the appropriateness, relevance, and ultimately the performance on a paper-pencil task. This basic project could easily be extended into other curriculum areas like writing and composition. Negotiation with the language arts teacher could lead to children writing essays about their experiences in this project and, thereby, strengthening the curriculum through integration. Group projects and individual assignments that require direct and simple application of the topic taught through direct instruction are common in a large class context. They enable the teacher to play the validator role effectively.

***Chalk Coloring and the Challenger Role***   Piaget (1953) asserts that growth and development cannot take place without cognitive conflict. Most constructivist educators see it as their primary role to stimulate appropriate cognitive conflict in their students in order to help them learn and develop. When done for the first time, chalk painting may be extremely challenging and frustrating. The chalk disappears from the paper frequently unless held together with hairspray. By the same token, a cognitive conflict created by the teacher to enable students to think is often irrelevant if not held together with a prior scheme. Darker chalk colors must be used first if we want the lighter colors to be seen. Constructed concepts must be anchored first before opportunities to restructure schemes are introduced. Since every individual operates at a different pace, large classes pose a unique problem to the challenger role. This is more so because a cognitive conflict differs from a problem/task designed with an increasing level of difficulty. Ideally, a cognitive conflict stimulates the construction of a new concept rather than validating a learned concept. The teacher deliberately poses a question to activate the students' schemes before introducing the new concept through direct instruction.

A teacher presents a problem to an 8th-grade class of 49 students. She points to the structure of the school building, which is an L-shaped block and an L-shaped concrete path that connects with the extreme ends of the building to form a quadrangle—a rectangular lawn—in the middle. This quadrangle is to be considered as deep water that one must not step into under any circumstance. Diagonally opposite to the inner corner of the L-shaped building is a tall coconut tree. The task for the students is to find a way to measure the diagonal distance between the coconut tree and the inner corner of the L-shaped building.

The teacher allows two groups of 8 to 9 students to step out at a time and use the given rope and measuring tapes to try out their

*The large class, by its very dynamics, provides an excellent opportunity for teachers to be effective scaffolds for children's learning since much of the thinking is done in peer groups. The inability to spend one-on-one time with each individual in the classroom proves to be an asset in that the temptation for the teacher to do things for the student is replaced with an effort to structure an activity to enable the student to follow through with his/her own construction of knowledge about the topic at hand.*

solutions. The remaining groups stay in to plan their strategies before it is their turn to go outside. Students begin to try a variety of methods and engage in measuring, throwing the rope from one end to the other, calculating and plotting their plans. When they return with their discoveries, the teacher scaffolds their ideas. She finds the right moment to re-introduce and validate concepts like perimeter, triangle, area from previous lessons. Finally, she introduces the topic that she has intended to teach all along—Pythagoras' Theorem. The lesson is complete and the class uses the fragmented measurements to check if the theorem actually works. The homework? To list uses that this theorem may have in real life.

Apart from the fact that such activities cater to a variety of learning styles, the time constraints that exist because of the large numbers may actually be an advantage. The time is just enough to stimulate thinking, try out a couple of ideas and be ready to understand the direct instruction as the teacher changes to the 'instructor role' from the 'challenger role'. The direct instruction, although distant from real life in this situation, becomes authentic and relevant because of the presented problem. Stigler and Stevenson (1991) note that in China and Japan, teachers often revolve lessons around one single problem and, thus, encourage mastery rather than fragmented understanding. We find this observation to be true of Indian teachers, too.

*Stenciling and the Guide Role*    Much as the stencil guides the artist's pencil and reveals the product on the paper when removed, teachers in large classes actively scaffold children by being strong, durable guides. A scaffold is effective only if the external assistance is just enough for the student to stand by him/herself. Unnecessary assistance can handicap learning by making the student completely dependent on the teacher thereby making it difficult for the teacher to withdraw from the situation (Diaz, Neal, & Amaya-Williams, 1990). The large class, by its very dynamics, provides an excellent opportunity for teachers to be effective scaffolds for children's learning since much of the thinking is done in peer groups. The inability to spend one-on-one time with each individual in the classroom proves to be an asset in that the temptation for the teacher to do things for the student is replaced with an effort to structure an activity to enable the student to follow through with his/her own construction of knowledge about the topic at hand. The teacher's effectiveness as a guide depends on the kind of stencil that he/she creates and the way in which classrooms are set up for effective peer interactions.

One of the 'stencils' that teachers in India commonly use is the homework assignment. Since parents are expected to supervise the homework, a well designed homework activity not only creates a strong scaffold for a child's learning but also serves to strengthen the interaction between a parent and the child. One of us, Pradnya Patet, remembers a childhood experience that illustrates this home-school connection through homework.

My 2nd-grade history teacher talked about the concept of 'unity in diversity' and how India had people of different religions, languages, colors and castes. We then talked about how each one of us was different. Next, we focused on the fact that we all had noses to breathe through, eyes to see, ears to hear and so on. The homework assignment required each student to draw a picture of anything that would represent unity in diversity. I recall sitting with my mom, brainstorming. The resulting list was a combination of her ideas and mine. I picked the idea that appealed the most to me: different kinds of fish living side by side in one fish tank. Once I started drawing, I wanted to find out about different kinds of fish because I needed to draw them. The next day in class, there were so many different drawings. From this activity, we moved into learning the pledge of India, a topic that probably would not have made much sense without this mediating activity.

Many teachers who seek to enhance knowledge construction in children probably do activities like this one. The uniqueness lies in the quality time that it facilitates between the parent and child. In addition, the teacher and parent can successfully withdraw from the situation and let the child stand alone because the teacher is physically non-existent and the parent does not face the time constraints that the teacher does in class. When time is restricted, even if the classroom is small, adults are tempted to do something for children rather than wait for them to come up with an idea on their own.

The art of effective teaching—whether in small or big classes—depends partly on how well the given homework ties in with a concept that has been taught and how concretely it is used as an anchor for the rest of the instruction. In large classrooms, homework becomes one of the popular ways to ensure the quality of learning since classroom time is not enough to accommodate each individual's pace. Done with a good balance between lower level and higher level thinking questions, strong connections between the instruction before and after the homework, and supervision from home, the mastery of learned concepts is enhanced.

*Blow Painting and the Weaver Role*  When blow painting, steering the paint by blowing through a straw directs the colors to flow into each other at intersecting points and weave an intricate pattern. A teacher, in turn, facilitates the flow of knowledge and helps students to extend their individual knowledge by building on each other's learning and simultaneously weaving a new body of knowledge. Peer tutoring is one of the effective strategies of constructivist teaching (Tudge, 1990). In many ways, in large classrooms, peer tutoring becomes a successful by-product of small group work and the inability of the teacher to handle large numbers.

After a spelling test in a 2nd-grade classroom, the teacher asks the students to exchange their books with their neighbors. "Use your red pencil to correct your friend's answers," the teacher directs. The students proceed to grade their peers' work. After the majority of the class has finished, the teacher instructs, "Now, explain to each other why you think some words are wrong and what might be the right spelling." As the students proceed to follow these directions, the teacher writes the correct spellings on the board. If there is any doubt or a student thinks that the peer has been unfair with the grading, both individuals proceed to the teacher's desk to voice their concerns and resolve the issue.

Although we question the use of spelling tests as a valid activity for knowledge construction (see e.g. Whitmore & Goodman, 1995), the way in which it is used for peer tutoring makes it an authentic activity. The opportunity to discuss errors and attempt to correct them with peer guidance places a different angle on the activity itself. It also explains why some research suggests that language arts and especially writing mechanics improve with specific structured schooling experiences rather than unorganized play (Cole, 1990; Gallimore & Tharp, 1990).

Guided grading of an assignment can prove to be a very effective assignment in itself. Correcting errors is a good way to improve one's own skills in a non-threatening environment. Other peer tutoring activities observed in large classrooms revolve around new concepts taught through direct instruction. A brief 5- to 10- minute period of peer tutoring immediately following direct instruction allows students to process the new information in their own way with guidance from each other.

***Still-life and the Model Role*** Still life art reproduces an object or a set of objects in a very realistic manner. The product however, varies according to the artist's interpretation of what he/she sees in the object. The teacher serves as a model to all students that he/she comes in contact with. The teacher often influences cultural values, thinking strategies and even handwriting. The following observation in a kindergarten classroom demonstrates how quickly children pick up behaviors and imitate a model in front of them.

Seventy kindergarteners were engaged in a game conducted by their teacher who phonetically spelt out a word and encouraged the children to perform the action. "J-u-mp – jump." One of the children jumped. The teacher nodded and jumped in her place. As she jumped the portion of her sari (the native dress of India—6 yards of cloth draped around the body in a specific way) on her shoulder began to fall off. She promptly put her hand on the shoulder to keep that part of the sari in place. In a little while, most of the kindergarteners were jumping with their hands on their shoulders.

This anecdote explains why teachers need to constantly be on the alert. The teacher is a model at all times. As we reminisced our own schooling experiences in preparation for this chapter, we recalled the amount of non-academic learning that occurred when we interacted with our teachers, listened to their stories and watched their actions. We found that we have internalized many of our teachers' values, beliefs and habits.

## A Masterpiece Emerges

The descriptions of practices and scenarios in this chapter highlight certain characteristics of large-class teaching in India. Although these characteristics stem partially from the constraints of managing a large group, close examination reveals that they are essential for constructivist-based teaching practice. Let us zoom in on this connection.

(a) *Teachers use many time-slots of structured guidance and/or direct instruction.* As we saw in the description of a typical school day, instruction is divided into 35-minute instruction time slots. Such structured guidance is important to help children crystallize the concepts that they have constructed. More specifically, adequate developmentally appropriate guidance is important for construction of schooled concepts (Cole, 1990). Unguided activity or play, on the other hand, generates a wide variety of opportunities for concrete learning but left at that level, fails to anchor the constructed concepts or extend them further towards practical application. As is evident from our anecdote of the teacher in the instructor role, much depends on how the structured guidance accommodates individual student needs, how the transition time is used to prepare children for direct instruction and how student interest is sustained through relevant examples rather than abstract conceptualizations.

(b) *Teachers focus on homework as an essential part of instruction, more specifically as a tool to validate learned concepts and stimulate schemas to be receptive to new instruction that is to follow.* Using homework as a teaching tool not only allows for individually paced learning but also provides a connecting point between school and home since parents are expected to supervise their children's homework. Such home-school continuity is beneficial for children (Bronfenbrenner, 1979; Bredekamp & Copple, 1997). Again, the appropriateness of homework depends on the teacher's ability to design it in a manner that allows the parent and child to work together successfully, limits it to a time span that is convenient for parents and developmentally appropriate for students and benefits all concerned by stimulating higher level thinking rather than rote memory.

(c) *Teachers present students with guided activity settings that involve group work and peer tutoring thereby tacitly communicating that the teacher and learner share the responsibility of learning.* Group activity and peer tutoring are desirable because they enhance knowledge construction by encouraging students to examine different points of view (Tudge, 1990; Moll & Greenberg, 1990). Our anecdotes in this chapter illustrate the use of groups, large and small, to enhance knowledge construction. More on cooperative learning is given by George Jacobs and Loh Wan Inn (see Chapter 10).

(d) *Teachers serve as direct and indirect models in order to promote behaviors that are culturally valued.* We saw that the canvas of cultural values and behaviors lays the foundation for the creation of the master-piece. It is clear that a teacher's role as a model goes beyond the prescribed syllabus and curriculum. Modeling culturally appro-priate behaviors provides students with a strong setting to construct their understanding of the socio-cultural context that they live in and a healthy opportunity to evaluate the basis of traditions for themselves.

(e) *Teachers form emotional bonds with children.* In classrooms that we refer to in this chapter, children usually sit in rows. Current thinking about physical arrangements might label this as most traditional and possibly non-constructivist. However, in large classes, such an arrangement is effective. The arrangement makes it easier for teachers to remember and learn the names of the children in a short span of time. It also helps the teacher to be aware of which children have not come to class. This makes children significant to the teacher. The seating arrangement enables the teacher to provide appropriate individual guidance in a systematic manner and not leave any children out. All this effort put into strengthening a one-to-one relationship creates an emotional bond that reinforces the cultural value of respect and reverence for the teacher. This emotional bonding makes a unique contribution to the teaching–learning process in the Indian context.

> *All this effort put into strengthening a one-to-one relationship creates an emotional bond that reinforces the cultural value of respect and reverence for the teacher. This emotional bonding makes a unique contribution to the teaching–learning process in the Indian context.*

## The Final Touches

In this chapter, we painted a picture with diverse classroom scenarios from India. We colored in some universal roles that teachers use when they mix and match methods and techniques with their knowledge about the learner's developmental patterns to accommodate the socio-cultural context. Developing the 'art' of teaching is a process that comes from the interaction between individual characteristics and environmental experiences. An artist creates a piece of art with a variety of tools and works with different textures of paper and colors of paint. As the colors and textures begin to merge with the artist's desires and plans, a picture emerges with a close connection between the materials and the creator's aspirations and knowledge about art. A teacher too, creates a community of learners with a variety of teaching strategies grounded in a theoretical philosophy and works with different learning styles, sub-cultures and family backgrounds. These unique experiences and abilities begin to merge with the teacher's desires, plans and knowledge of the subject matter. Learning emerges with a close connection between the students and the teacher as the cyclical nature of the teaching-learning process becomes evident. The 'art' of teaching large classes continually evolves as teachers strive to challenge themselves to reach out to each individual, converting the constraints to advantages, and polishing their masterpiece with reflective practice, reconstructed methods, and a unique signature that incorporates their style and personality.

# References

Bajpayee, K.D. (1988). Pracheen Bhartia kala me Guru Shishya. In Kalyan (Ed.), *Shiksha ank* (Vol. 1, pp. 264-267). Gorakhpur, India: Geeta Press.

Berk, L. E., & Winsler, A. (1995). *Scaffolding children's learning: Vygotsky and early childhood education.* Washington, D.C.: NAEYC

Bredekamp, S., & Copple, C. (Eds.). (1997). *Developmentally appropriate practice in early childhood programs* (Rev. ed.). Washington, D.C.: NAEYC.

Bredekamp, S., & Rosegrant, T. (Eds.). (1995). *Reaching potentials: Transforming early childhood curriculum and assessment* (Vol. 2). Washington, D.C.: NAEYC

Bronfenbrenner, U. (1979). *The ecology of human development.* Cambridge, MA: Harvard University Press.

Cole, M. (1990). Cognitive development and schooling. In L. C. Moll (Ed.), *Vygotsky and education* (pp. 89-110). New York: Cambridge University Press.

Diaz, R. M., Neal, C. J., & Amaya-Williams, M. (1990). The social origins of self-regulation. In L. C. Moll (Ed.), *Vygotsky and education* (pp. 127-154). New York: Cambridge University Press.

Gallimore, R., & Tharp, R. (1990). Teaching mind in society. In L. C. Moll (Ed.), *Vygotsky and education* (pp. 175-205). New York: Cambridge University Press.

Moll, L. C., & Greenberg, J. B. (1990). Creating zones of possibilities. In L. C. Moll (Ed.), *Vygotsky and education* (pp. 319-348). New York: Cambridge University Press.

Mosteller, F. (1995). The Tennessee study of class size in the early school grades. *The Future of Children, 5*(2), 113-127.

Muralidharan, R., & Pankajam, G. (1988). *An evaluation study of the different models of preschool teacher training programs from the point of their impact on children.* New Delhi, India: NCERT.

Narain (1964). Growing up in India. *Family Process, 3*(1), 127-54.

Piaget, J. (1953). *The origins of intellect.* London: Routledge & Kegan Paul.

Piaget, J. (1965). *The moral judgement of the child.* Riverside, NJ: The Free Press.

Samaras, A. P. (2000). Scaffolding preservice teachers' learning. In N. J. Yelland (Ed.), *Promoting meaningful learning* (pp.17-24). Washington, D.C.: NAEYC

Saraswathi, T. S., & Dutta, R.(1988). *Invisible boundaries: Grooming for adult roles.* New Delhi, India: Northern Book Center.

Shantiniketan Vishwabharti Vishwavidyalaya, (1954). Guru Shishya pracheen sambandh stapith huye bina shiksha ka vikas sambhav nahi (an excerpt from Jawaharlal Nehru's convocation speech). In Kalyan (Ed.), *Shiksha ank* (Vol. 1, pp. 389-391). Gorakhpur, India: Geeta Press.

Stigler, J. W., & Stevenson, H. W. (1991). How Asian teachers polish each lesson to perfection. In E.N. Junn & Botatzis, C.J. (Eds.), *Annual editions, child growth and development 2000/2001.* Guilford, CT: Dushkin/McGraw Hill

Tudge, J. (1990). Vygotsky, the zone of proximal development, and peer collaboration: Implications for classroom practice. In L. C. Moll (Ed.), *Vygotsky and education* (pp. 155-172). New York: Cambridge University Press.

Whitmore, K. F., & Goodman, Y. M. (1995). Transforming curriculum in language and literacy. In S. Bredekamp & T. Rosegrant (Eds.), *Reaching potentials: Transforming early childhood curriculum and assessment* (Vol. 2, pp.145-166). Washington, D.C.: NAEYC

Woolfolk, A. (1998). *Educational Psychology.* Boston: Allyn and Bacon.

## About the Authors

**Pradnya Patet**, Ph D, serves as a faculty associate at Arizona State University, Tempe, Arizona. Prior to this, she was an assistant professor of Psychology and Early Childhood Education at Mount St. Clare College, Iowa, U.S.A. She grew up in India and moved to the United States of America as a young adult. Pradnya Patet writes and presents about cultural differences in teaching and learning, indigenous teaching and learning styles and universal theoretical principles that all cultures use despite the diversity in their practical applications. Her current research focuses on young children's understanding of classroom rules, its relationship with cooperative play and group games; and personality types on constructivist teaching styles. E-mail: p.patet@worldnet.att.net

**Meera Oke**, Ph D, is currently with the Film and TV Institute of India as an independent researcher documenting and analyzing experiments in theatre and performing arts from a Child Development perspective. She writes for a children's website and paper media on "Children's Games and Street Games" and conducts workshops on using theatre for cultural intervention with children, focusing on Theatre for Life Skills. Earlier, as a professor of Human Development and Family Relations, she was involved with teacher preparation, research and curriculum development in several universities in India. Meera Oke's research interests range from children's play and classroom practices to cross-cultural, multidisciplinary studies on global health, stigma and so on. Her work has led her to travel to South Africa, China, the United States of America and countries in Europe. E-mail: udaymira@pn2.vsnl.net.in

# CHAPTER 4

# Teaching Large Classes in the Waldorf Schools

*Richard Blunt*

The Waldorf Schools are widely known by reputation as schools that cater to the interests of parents who want their children to have an education that develops their individuality, creativity and critical thinking. However, few people outside those teachers who are trained in Waldorf methodology understand its theoretical basis. Misconceptions abound (Blunt, 1999), despite its longstanding successful history. The purpose of this chapter is to provide an introduction to the Waldorf approach and illustrate its values for teaching large classes in diverse settings. It is expected that the chapter will be of interest to those teachers who seek a deeper dimension to their teaching, and who are prepared to experiment creatively in making their classrooms more challenging for their pupils, not only intellectually, but holistically through emotional and physical expression.

## The Waldorf Approach to Education

Waldorf schools use the arts as media for integrating the content (knowledge, skills and attitudes) and deepening learners' understanding of the curriculum. For this reason, their approach is sometimes termed "art-based education". They have developed separately from conventional school systems, which tend to be "information-based". Despite—or perhaps because of—their separate status, they constitute the largest independent school movement in the world. There are more than 600 registered Waldorf schools in 42 countries on all five continents (Maher and Bleach, 1997). These Waldorf schools are distinct from the Rudolf Steiner schools for mentally challenged children and from the kindergartens. They are for children of normal abilities and they make no distinctions between children in terms of race, gender, religion or social class.

The schools were established on the basis of guidance given by Rudolf Steiner (1861-1925), an Austrian philosopher. Steiner developed his theory of human development from his own experience of teaching. Although he did so without the benefit of the findings of contemporary cognitive psychology, his conclusions accord closely with some of the most influential theories of intellectual development. An indication of the similarities will be given later in this chapter.

*International Endorsement*   With relevance to the theme of this book, UNESCO's International Commission on Education for the 21st Century endorsed the Waldorf approach as follows: "the originality of this educational approach and its longstanding practical application all over the world have recently proved to be particularly interesting and fruitful in such disadvantaged environments as slums, refugee camps, or in conflict situations, conditions where alternative channels of education often prove to be more efficient than official school systems" (Maher and Shepherd, 1995, Appendix 2). The report cites as examples: African township schools in Soweto, South Africa; a refugee school in the Gaza strip; a school in Brazil for street children; a Belfast school that admits children from both Catholic and Protestant families; and a South Dakota Reservation school for children of Sioux Indian families. Typically, such schools have too few teachers, each of whom needs to take responsibility for large classes of children, and meagre resources. Moreover, the children are often not accustomed to the modes of teaching and learning that are practised in conventional schools. Such children require an education system that reaches out to the culture of their families and communities, taking into consideration their need for holistic learning that challenges their physical, emotional and intellectual energies.

Not that Waldorf schools specifically target impoverished conditions. Indeed, Waldorf education serves the interests of all socioeconomic classes because its artistic principles are universal and can be implemented with the simplest resources. Waldorf teachers create artistic opportunities for children to learn. Using the arts of dance, song, stories, poetry, painting, sculpture and so on, teachers are able to present all the subjects of the traditional curriculum in ways that integrate learning and provide children with opportunities for spiritual expression and fulfillment.

*An Anecdote*   My first experience of a family who sent their children to a Waldorf school is apposite. Unable to have their own children, the couple had decided to adopt a 2-year-old boy who had a history of abuse. Initially fearful, timid and withdrawn, the child soon began to project his traumas onto other children. He behaved so aggressively that no nursery school would admit him. Over the course of the next few years, they took him to the best child psychologists in the country, but nothing seemed to help. When they tried to register him at a school, they would have to take him out within hours because he attacked his classmates, sometimes with stones. They had exhausted all avenues of help—or so they thought—when a friend suggested they take him to the local Waldorf School. They had never heard of the school or the school system, but on the friend's recommendation they applied. When the school admitted the boy, they were fully aware of his history but placed him directly in a large class. The child's aggressive behaviour soon began to emerge, but the teacher focussed on leading the class through activities that would help him to express his repressed feelings. After two days, there was no further evidence of his previous behaviour. With the exception of a few instances of temper, it never returned. When I met the boy, he was a healthy and cheerful 12-year-old with a strong character. Although he enjoyed the Waldorf School, he was looking forward to moving to a conventional school after completing the primary phase because he wanted more opportunities to play sport.

The point of this story is not that Waldorf Schools can effect miracle healings—although in this case the effects were dramatic—but that when the principles of arts-based education are properly understood and applied they can have a profound effect, even (or especially) with large classes. Children such as the boy mentioned above become part of a joyful, physically and emotionally active group of children who are learning well because they are fully involved, body and soul. In many conventional schools that I have visited, the teachers are either unaware of the value of art, or else they become "precious" about it, trying to make the children imitate adult forms of art. For example, instead of singing songs with rhythm, melody, mood and interesting lyrics, the teachers choose songs that are too sophisticated and boring. The result is that children grow up in the belief that art is inappropriate for their lives.

***Child-centred Perspectives***   In the last 3 decades, conventional education systems have adopted the view that teachers should provide children with opportunities to learn from a variety of resources. The theory behind this view is child-centred, that it is the child who is doing the learning, not the teacher, so teachers should not "interfere" with learning, but should rather "facilitate" it. In the words of Carl Rogers, "A way must be found to develop a climate in the *system* in which the focus is not upon *teaching*, but on the facilitation of self-directed *learning*" (Rogers, 1969, p.304). One of the proponents of this perspective, John Holt, argued that conventional schooling alienates children from learning by forcing them to differentiate it from play. Instead of preserving children's natural enthusiasm for learning, schools train them to perceive it as something that is "exchanged for grades, praise, approval, success, to be measured, evaluated..." (Holt, 1972, p.253).

Waldorf teachers would be sympathetic to such a view, but not to the implication that is often deduced from it: that teachers necessarily "interfere" when they become personally involved in children's learning. If the teacher's task were merely to ensure that children develop the *techniques* of reading, writing and arithmetic without paying attention to what these skills mean in their lives, such an implication might be plausible. However, if teachers are to integrate intellectual, emotional and physical education, make it relevant, and establish the foundations of creativity and freedom in the child's life, the character and abilities of the teacher as well as the teacher's relationship with the children become vital elements of classroom practice.

*This is the challenge for the Waldorf teacher: not merely to leave the child with "self-directed learning" in the hope that creativity, self-esteem and innate abilities would somehow spontaneously emerge, but to challenge, awaken and develop the child's social and spiritual potentials through artistic activities.*

This is the challenge for the Waldorf teacher: not merely to leave the child with "self-directed learning" in the hope that creativity, self-esteem and innate abilities somehow spontaneously emerge, but to challenge, awaken and develop the child's social and spiritual potentials through artistic activities. Such goals take more than superficial technique to achieve. For the education of the child's inner life—the range and depth of their feelings, the power of their will, and their ability to think imaginatively—teachers need an understanding of the stages of physical and mental maturation through which they pass, together with the qualities of the relationships and activities needed for education at each stage.

This chapter outlines the principles of Waldorf education: its perspectives on child development; its view of holistic development; and its principles of teaching that aim to enable children to develop a deep sense of self understanding and freedom. On this basis, the potential of the approach for teaching large classes, while preserving a deep personal relationship between teacher and pupil, is explained and illustrated.

## Child Development

The principles and practices of Waldorf education are developed from Rudolf Steiner's analysis of the stages of child development. Therefore, in order to explain the ways in which Waldorf teachers are able to manage large classes of children, a brief overview of this analysis will be given. For the reader who is unfamiliar with Steiner's work, perhaps the best way to explain it is by comparing it to the theory of instruction developed by the educationist Jerome Bruner (1971).

*A Comparison with Bruner*  Drawing on the research of Piaget and others, Bruner identified three stages in the process of intellectual development whereby children free themselves from immediate responses to the world and learn to "mediate" their responses. The first stage was characterized by "knowing how to do", in which the child learned to translate information received into physical action. Bruner called this the "enactive mode of representation." In the second stage, the child learned to represent information more internally and reflectively in the form of images or "iconic representation". In this stage, the child used both enactive and iconic representation. In the third stage, which was associated with the onset of puberty (although the link to hormonal change could not be explained), language became the primary medium of thought. This he named "symbolic representation". Bruner considered that although by the third stage the child was able to use all three modes of representation, the best order in which to learn anything was to begin with the enactive mode, then move to iconic and finally to the symbolic: from action to image to language.

Bruner's concern was to identify the most efficient and effective route to intellectual development. He argued that intellectual development could be speeded up and the quality of the child's understanding strengthened if the teacher were to follow the sequence from action to image to language in each learning task. Rudolf Steiner was not concerned with speed. He believed that children had particular qualities that needed to be developed in the appropriate stages of development, and that teachers would only do children a disservice if they attempted to hurry them through to intellectual maturity. The role of the teacher was to ensure that the child's potentials in each stage were challenged and developed in holistic ways.

Steiner's interpretation of the stages was less intellectual than Bruner's. In addition, Steiner believed that the changes in the ways children experience the world (such as those described by Bruner) were indeed linked to physiological changes that occurred around the ages of 7 (associated with the change of teeth) and 14 (puberty).

**Childhood**    Steiner considered that the first stage was dominated by imitation. The child's impulses of will (Drever, 1952) were expressed through the limbs (Bruner's "enactive mode"). For Steiner, the will was not merely a concept but an energy that dominated the child's strong motivation to learn in the first period of life. Following Schopenhauer, Steiner taught that the will was unconscious and worked subliminally through imitation, developing the abilities of language, walking, dexterity, etc. through repetition (in contrast to conscious practice). When the limbs were exercised, energies of the will flowed upwards through the limbs and torso towards the head, and teachers could begin to educate these energies using conscious rhythmical movement, especially activities imbued with feeling (see below: the temperaments). Rhythm, music and colour were the elements of art that could "speak to" the will and feelings, and draw them into union with thinking.

In the second stage (between the change of teeth and puberty) the child's imitative powers (in which what is observed is directly assimilated) transform into the ability to create and remember images (Bruner's iconic mode). These images were dynamic in character. Steiner used the term "*bildlich*", which suggested not only the pictorial but also the idea of modeling, fashioning, creative industry (Steiner, 1968). For Steiner, feelings arose from the interaction between unconscious forces of the will flowing upwards into the torso, and conscious forces of thinking flowing downwards through the head. "Feelings" were what we experience as the meeting of these forces in the area of the chest. They were "semi-conscious" because they were a mixture between unconscious will and conscious thinking. The challenge for the teacher was to ensure a strong and harmonious union between them, and again, the best educational medium to achieve this integration was art. Thus, the teacher was to further develop the use of songs, stories and drama, especially myths, which were imbued with truth in the form of imagery.

Images such as those in fairy tales were not to be used merely instrumentally. Adults had to really believe in the inner wisdom of the tale or myth because if they did not, children would sense the adults' insincerity and in consequence would develop distrust and cynicism for ideas and people. Such feelings were inappropriate because it was at this stage of life that the child learned trust and reverence. Given opportunities to develop these qualities in this stage, individuals would have them for their whole lives, but deprived of this opportunity they would experience them only feebly in later life. To inspire reverence for authority, the teacher should appear to children as a wise and trustworthy authority who was deserving of emulation. If children were able to trust and revere a teacher as a moral, consistent authority in this stage, they themselves would develop into strong integrated characters, able to inspire trust in others. In the second stage, therefore, the unconscious imitation of the early years should develop into a healthy feeling for authority.

**Puberty**   In the third stage, associated with puberty, children develop self-awareness. They gradually become able to objectify, identify and control their will and feelings. In so doing they are able to transform what they previously learned in the form of images (e.g. moral principles) into abstract concepts that are independent of images, and thence to verbalise them (Bruner's "symbolic mode") (Blunt, 1999). Art should remain the guiding principle for education in adolescence, retaining the emphasis on integrating the forces of the will and thinking by developing a strong emotional life. However, it was important not to rush children into this phase. Rather, they should develop clear understandings of their feelings and attitudes in terms of opposites (love-hate, good-bad), and strong aesthetic feelings (beautiful-ugly). They should learn to associate the beautiful with the good, which would give them an integrated emotional foundation for their moral life. These approaches would invigorate their feelings, whereas subtle, confusing and ambivalent feelings at this stage would enervate them both physically and intellectually.

The principle that Steiner emphasized was that our educational methods should be based on our knowledge of physiological and psychological development, rather than on our ideas about how we think education ought to take place. "It is not for us to decide according to our likes or dislikes what kind of education should be given to our children.... Education should rather be dictated by the needs of human nature itself" (Steiner, 1966, p.126).

Besides the stages of development, another "dictate of nature" that teachers take into account in Waldorf Education is the notion of temperament. This underpins the emotional character of the child, and will be explained and related to Steiner's view of development in the following section.

## Temperament

Steiner considered that one of a teacher's more challenging tasks was to help children develop their character. In conventional education, "character" is taken as a given—good, bad or indifferent—and teachers have little idea of what they can do to help develop it. Thus, they are often judgmental when children do not behave in accordance with their expectations. Steiner argued that what we understand as character was an expression of temperament.

He used the Classical Greek description of the temperaments to explain—and help teachers to work with—individual differences between children. The closest contemporary approach to temperaments can be found in the research into "learning styles" (Kolb, 1976; Honey and Mumford, 1982). However, learning styles as described by these authors focus on cognitive differences between learners and have no theory to explain how they arise. By contrast, Steiner's use of the temperaments was holistic, emphasizing individual differences between people. The four temperaments are the phlegmatic, sanguine, choleric and melancholic.

The temperaments provide a holistic approach to individuality in terms of Steiner's view of development. (The following account is summarized from Blunt 1999, pp.96-99.) Steiner explained that the temperaments arise when one of the four members of the human being (the ego, the physical body, the forces of thinking and of will) dominates the others. If the physical dimension dominates, the melancholic temperament arises. If the ego dominates, the choleric temperament asserts itself. Over-predominance of the forces of thinking results in the phlegmatic temperament, and the sanguine temperament comes from excessive forces of will. The goal of the teacher is to both develop all four members and to bring them into balance.

***Developing the Temperaments***   The development of the temperaments is achieved by associating them with certain qualities of movement, music and images. The choleric temperament is associated with strong, goal directed steps. By contrast, phlegmatic movements are slow and comfortable, with little expression. Sanguine movements are mobile, cheerful, with little direction, and melancholic movements are gloomy. In terms of music, the choleric temperament is attracted to strident, martial music whereas the phlegmatic prefers peaceful, gentle tones. The melancholic loves sad, emotional melodies while the sanguine prefers quick, happy tunes and varied rhythms. There are also character-types associated with the temperaments. These are given in the form of archetypal images of the four temperaments, as expressed in stories, fables and myths. With young children, anthropomorphism (using animal characters in fables to represent the different temperaments) is used to caricature a temperament. For example, a lion might represent the choleric temperament, birds the sanguine, a hippo the phlegmatic, and a bloodhound the melancholic.

By clearly differentiating and caricaturing the temperaments, Waldorf teachers are able to develop their pupils' understanding of the elements of their inner soul nature. Steiner emphasized that this was not merely a conceptual theory, but could be confirmed empirically by introspection and experiment. As teachers used movements, music and images associated with the different temperaments, they would see how different children were attracted and their attention gained when they experience their own temperament in qualities of movement, music and images. Whereas some teachers believed that their responsibility was to suppress qualities such as the choleric tendency to aggressive self-assertion, Steiner found that these excesses were best treated by reflecting the temperament back to the child in a way that would enable the child to see its results. In this way, teachers need to think homeopathically, using the principle that like moderates like: "Not only can like be known by like, but like can be treated and healed by like." (Steiner, 1947, p.82). For this reason, children who exhibit similar temperaments are grouped together in class.

A teacher demonstrated this principle to me as follows. He told his class (of 7- and 8-year-olds) a story of a stray dog that stole a string of sausages from a shop. Having grouped together children of like temperament, the teacher indicated to me one corpulent child who he said was strongly phlegmatic, interested mainly in his own comforts and not in class work. Indeed, even as the teacher was speaking, the boy was rummaging in his satchel for a sandwich. It was to capture the interest of this child that he brought in a strong "food" theme, which attracted the interest of phlegmatics because of its comforting properties. He began his story by describing the stray dog wandering aimlessly but cheerfully around town (the sanguine temperament). Next, he told how the dog smelled the delicious aroma of the sausages drifting down the street. At this, the phlegmatic child, who was dozing, pricked up his ears. The dog followed the aroma from street to street until she found a mountain of plump sausages in a butcher's window. She stole a string of sausages and was chased by the irate butcher (the choleric temperament). Unfortunately, the butcher caught and relieved the dog of her prize, leaving her sad and disappointed (the melancholic temperament). The attention of the phlegmatic child had been captured and held by the story without the teacher needing to demand and enforce it.

*The Temperaments in Large Classes*　When dealing with large classes, knowledge of these inner processes that motivate children is of inestimable value for capturing and keeping their attention. Besides holding their interest, this knowledge is important for creating classroom discipline. Teachers who understand that children's attention is not merely attracted by novel information but rather by activities, music and images that are rich with the moods that are associated with the temperaments, are able to influence children much more strongly. Not only does knowledge of the temperaments enable teachers to hold the attention of large classes, but it also helps teachers to calm and focus their attention. As long as children are in a sad, angry, distracted or over-relaxed mood, they will be unable to concentrate on learning, but as the teacher is able to work with their temperaments they quickly settle down.

So powerful are the dynamics associated with the temperaments that it is of great importance that teachers learn to balance their own temperaments. A choleric teacher, for example, will create anxiety in the class and this will affect the physical well being of the children. By contrast, teachers with balanced temperaments are able to reflect the various temperaments to the pupils in various artistic ways, through music, movement and story telling.

Everyone has a mix of temperaments, and each stage of life has a characteristic temperament, so teachers should look for trends rather than extreme types. Young children are generally sanguine, whereas the adolescent temperament is choleric. In maturity people become melancholic and in old age phlegmatic (Steiner, 1967).

## Methodology

The challenge for Waldorf teachers to stimulate holistic development means that they plan each lesson to integrate (1) physical activity (which stimulates the will), (2) rhythms and harmonies of music, colour, form and language (which involve the feelings), and (3) imaginative ideas such as narrative and imagery (which evoke pictorial thinking) (Blunt, 1999). In other words, the teacher's practical maxim is to involve "hand, heart and head" in that order, in the same way as Bruner encouraged the order of enactive, iconic and symbolic activities for developing concepts. Art provides the basis for achieving integration. For example, a lesson in simple division might be planned to begin actively, with the learners collecting pebbles and dividing them into equal groups of a particular size. This might be followed by a story or song emphasizing the value of being able to divide a large number of things into smaller groups of equal size. The teacher might also have the children illustrate the story or song in a painting. The same principles are maintained in the more senior classes, although obviously with increasing levels of technical and conceptual sophistication. Finally, the class might chant an appropriate multiplication table by heart.

*Creativity and Integrity*   Although there are principles for teaching, there are no prescribed lessons. Teachers must devise their own unique lessons using the principles to guide them. This ensures that teachers are creatively involved with their teaching and are able to improvise, adjust and develop their plans. The point has already been made that the Waldorf teacher is able to practice these principles even in large classes and at all levels. Materials can be simple so this is not an approach that only the wealthy can afford. Waldorf schools work with the materials available to them. For example, if there are no flutes and drums, the children make rattles, clap, stamp their feet, whistle and hum.

Waldorf schools use religious, mythic and folk-tale imagery which appeals to children's imaginations. Every culture is rich with characters embedded in history, folklore and fables, and they make a profound impression on the young imagination. In the European tradition, the tales of the Grimm brothers are especially valued for this purpose. The morals that are usually embedded in such tales and characters should not be abstracted and made explicit, but rather left implicit. The child's sense of rationality will work on the images, and at the right time—after puberty—they will transform the activity or moral from living image to abstract concept for themselves. Children love a good story, whether in large or small classes, and Waldorf teachers practise story telling during their training so that they are able to absorb their class in each story.

Before puberty, the task of the Waldorf teacher is to help the child develop thinking and feeling and willing in an integrated way. This is best achieved by using the arts, because art engages the imagination, feeling and physical activity (the will). Besides developing an understanding of their feelings (so neglected in conventional schools), the integration of the processes of thinking, feeling and willing enables children to develop their powers of concentration and memory, and thereby they are able to enjoy learning more, even with the distractions that large classes bring. Again, Steiner emphasized that this was not to be hurried. The energies of the soul should be stimulated and challenged but not forced to emerge.

The integrity of the teacher is crucial for the success of education. Hence, teachers who wished to enable children to develop strong intellectual, emotional and moral qualities had to approach all their work with love, truthfulness, grace and imagination.

***Experiencing Freedom*** Steiner maintained that the powers of imitation that hold sway in the first 7 years of childhood evolve into a need for authority after the change of teeth (Blunt, 1999). This need must be fulfilled if children are to develop properly into adolescence, because it is then that children learn to experience freedom. That is, children can only develop true independence when it is founded on true dependence. True dependence is acceptance of the authority of trustworthy adults who have not attempted to impose their personal ideas and values but have given their knowledge in artistic form (through stories, pictures, music, songs, drama, dance and movement). If there are intellectual ideas to be learned at this stage (such as the alphabet, numbers, multiplication tables, names of plants, animals, countries etc.) they should be memorized (accepted on trust) rather than assimilated by reasoning. When, after puberty, the powers of reason and abstraction awaken, children experience freedom and independence as they discover for themselves the symbolic truths embedded in the artistic forms of the earlier stage. Each discovery has a deepening and strengthening effect on their intellectual lives as they experience the power of symbolic thinking in language.

**Authority and Repetition**   The principles of authority and memorization have strong implications for teaching large classes. The most obvious is that Waldorf teachers establish unusually close relationships with the children in their classes. Contemporary views of education that emphasize resource-based learning sometimes seek to devalue the role of the teacher in the process of learning. By contrast, Waldorf teachers are integral to every classroom activity, not in an imposing way, but in their role of introducing and leading artistic activities. In order to establish this close relationship from the beginning of every day, Waldorf teachers stand at the doors of their classrooms to greet each child by name as they enter, and insist that they make eye contact. This closeness is maintained throughout the day. Special efforts are made to bring the children's parents to the school and involve them in school activities, such as seasonal festivals and fêtes. This relationship between the teacher, child and family enables the teacher to gain deep influence in the child's life, and in large classes it enables the teacher to personalize every lesson to a considerable degree.

> *Waldorf teachers establish unusually close relationships with the children in their classes. In order to establish this close relationship from the beginning of every day, Waldorf teachers stand at the doors of their classrooms to greet each child by name as they enter, and insist that they make eye contact. This closeness is maintained throughout the day.*

The principle that memorization is the appropriate approach to learning between the change of teeth and puberty brings a new dynamic to the large class. It is not that Waldorf teachers suppress "why" questions at this stage, but rather that they reflect the questions, encouraging children to reason for themselves. In this way, children learn to reason when they are ready to do so and then they experience reasoning as an exciting challenge, rather than as drudgery. Therefore, the teacher's task is to present the content of lessons in artistic ways and show children how they can become involved in the artistic processes of creation. The processes of presentation and activity alternate so that the children are not bored, but learn to anticipate new developments. Waldorf classrooms are sometimes noisy with singing, chanting and music, and sometimes quiet with focused painting or modeling. Teachers orchestrate this variety and integration using the principles described, and are thereby able to keep many children actively involved in learning with feeling and will. This rhythm should not change when dealing with large classes. Noise is not seen as disruptive but as an expression of feeling and energy, which are integral to the processes of living and learning in childhood.

Unlike traditional education, which has come to eschew repetition, activities that develop the memory are considered valuable in Waldorf education. Similarly, the development of artistic talents such as singing, playing a musical instrument, movement, painting and modeling is valued as fundamental to education. Through the renewing influences of art, learning becomes invigorated. Viewed from the artistic perspective, intellectual development is not an end in itself, but integral to emotional and physical learning. Indeed, for the Waldorf teacher, strong, imaginative thinking develops out of meaningful feelings and activities. Therefore, teaching a large class in a Waldorf classroom means involving the class in appropriate artistic activities.

*Holistic Teaching* While conventional education ignores the harmonious development of the body, emotions and intellect, Waldorf education views it as essential to enable children to realise their full potential. For example, conventional education systems tend to view art as an elective subject, whereas Waldorf schools make it integral to every subject in the curriculum. Art is the principle that stimulates the memory and creates interest, involvement and motivation, enabling children to see the applications and relevance of each subject. In the more senior classes the emphasis on the imagination is maintained, but increasingly children are encouraged to think about applications of the disciplines in trades and professions.

Such activities are best achieved through group work in which children can pool their experience. By structuring group activities around an artistic task, the pupils are encouraged to work together creatively. For example, the group might be asked to create a scale landscape from a map, or develop a model of a bridge, recording what they need to know in terms of proportions and calculations. Such absorbing tasks can be done equally easily in large and small classes because the challenge of the task creates its own discipline.

The coherence and integration of the curriculum is achieved through geography. Steiner taught that geography should not be "regimented into a strictly demarcated timetable", but used as "a great channel into which everything flows and from which a great deal can also be derived" (Steiner, 1976, pp. 162-163). Mathematics can be used for mapping; Geology for the formation of the landscape; Botany and Zoology for the natural histories of plants, animals and humans; and social, economic, linguistic and cultural developments can be explained in relation to geographical settings. In large classes, one of the challenges is for pupils to develop an understanding of the curriculum that is self-sustaining so that the teacher does not need to constantly assist individuals who are behind the others. By developing an integrated curriculum around geography, Waldorf Schools provide children with strongly contextualized, meaningful knowledge which assists both understanding and memory.

## The Teacher's Authority

Authority is the crux of the teacher-pupil relationship in Waldorf schools. If authority fails, then teaching is no longer effective. Unfortunately, in recent years, the abuse of authority in education has led to bad publicity for the teaching profession, sometimes to the point where teachers are strongly constrained against imposing any degree of demand on children. The nature of authority that Rudolf Steiner encouraged was that of the master rather than the disciplinarian. Teachers have to earn the child's respect and "discipleship" through their deep concern for each individual, as well as out of respect for their knowledge and artistic ability. Thus, the teacher leads the class, directing the children not with force but through the strength of relationships they establish with them.

In most conventional schools, teachers specialize in a particular age group which means that the class must move to a new teacher at the end of each grade. However, in Waldorf Schools each class stays with the same teacher throughout the primary phase (7 years). Although this is challenging for both teachers and children, it enables teachers to establish an unusually deep relationship with the pupils and their families. This close relationship ensures that, on the one hand, pupils and their families can expect a high level of responsibility from their teacher, and on the other, that the teacher has a great deal of influence in each child's life. As teachers develop this relationship with the children and their families, earning respect through their competence and professional dedication, their authority in the classroom increases. In one large, diverse class I observed a teacher who had been with his class for 6 years, and was easily able to control their behaviour:

> As the children begin to complete their writing exercise, the noise in the class increases considerably. The teacher explains that this noise provides an important balance in a lesson. To begin with he kept the children under strong control (during his lesson). Then he released them to work on their own, and they have now swung to the other extreme of a lack of control. This rhythm is necessary in a lesson for the development and release of tension, or concentration followed by relaxation. However, it is vital that the teacher should not have to shout at his class in order to bring it under control again. He must be able to bring them together through their own free respect of his authority. By way of demonstration he simply walks to the front and begins an inconspicuous, rhythmical combination of clapping and clicking his fingers. In their own time the children put away their work, and one by one they join in, until the whole class is following the changing rhythms with complete concentration.
>
> Blunt, 1999, p.173

The teacher of this class used no textbooks. Instead, everything was given either concretely, for example by presenting a map or rock to study, or though his own descriptions and stories in which he was able to express his knowledge, imagination and feelings. He had developed his own book of fables, each artistically illustrated by himself, which served as the child's first reader. The goal of this approach was to prevent the dilution of the teacher's authority by an external authority, and to instill in children the value of learning from a human authority. Through this experience they would gain respect both for knowledge and for the process of education, which would sustain their motivation to learn from future teachers.

The teacher explained that Waldorf teachers do not indulge in praise because that merely flatters. By contrast, the child's enduring self-confidence develops from a sense of mastery which depends upon good teaching and learning.

Establishing the authority of the teacher is important for teaching large classes in any school system, but in the Waldorf approach it is essential because so little "force" is used. Everything in Waldorf

*Authority is the crux of the teacher-pupil relationship in Waldorf schools. If authority fails, then teaching is no longer effective. The nature of authority that Rudolf Steiner encouraged was that of the master rather than the disciplinarian. Teachers have to earn the child's respect and "discipleship" through their deep concern for each individual, as well as out of respect for their knowledge and artistic ability. Thus, the teacher leads the class, directing the children not with force but through the strength of relationships they establish with them.*

education depends on pupils accepting and respecting the teacher as leader and role model. On that basis, the powerful childhood instinct for imitation enables the child to develop the confidence that is the basis for a strong will (not mere willfulness), achieve emotional maturity, and be capable of imaginative thinking. By contrast, teachers who depend on threats and flattery to maintain control of a class alienate and lose the respect of the children, and with that goes any chance that they will be able to educate holistically.

## Class and School Management

Steiner considered teaching to be an art in the full sense of the word. He condemned the view that teaching was common sense, and instead tried to identify from his own experience the knowledge and abilities that teachers needed in order to be effective educators. Although Waldorf teachers undergo thorough training, Steiner emphasized the importance of providing support for them. Every Waldorf School has a College of Teachers in which the teachers discuss their work with their classes, receive support from their colleagues, and become part of the on-going development programme of the school. Teachers with large classes cannot be left to struggle in isolation. They need the interaction and interest of their colleagues to keep alive their creative energy and assist them both physically and spiritually.

*Every Waldorf School has a College of Teachers in which the teachers discuss their work with their classes, receive support from their colleagues, and become part of the on-going development programme of the school. Teachers with large classes cannot be left to struggle in isolation. They need the interaction and interest of their colleagues to keep alive their creative energy and assist them both physically and spiritually.*

The College of Teachers has a collegial rather than a supervisory function. Indeed, there are no entrenched posts for principals and heads of departments in Waldorf Schools. A Council of Management is elected to administer each school, comprising usually three parents and three teachers, and the Chair is appointed each year by consensus of the full College (Blunt, 1999). This arrangement is not easy, but it provides the best basis for teachers to learn to work together cooperatively as equals. The more experienced teachers mentor the less experienced.

As explained above, the ideal is that a single teacher will take a class through the whole of primary school. However, this does not rule out contributions from specialist teachers for foreign languages, music, specific religious denominations and so on. Many Waldorf teachers only regard teachers as "qualified" when they have taken one class through the full primary phase. At the secondary level each class has a class teacher for the main lesson (see below), but increasing use is made of specialist teachers, many of whom need to be able to modify their methods to present both the Waldorf curriculum as well as that for the state examinations. Arrangements to handle these challenges vary, with some schools attempting to integrate the curricula and others dealing with the Waldorf curriculum in the mornings and the state requirements in the afternoons.

Each day, the class has a lengthy (usually 2 hours) main lesson with a clear theme, in which the pupils are taken artistically through the stages of awakening the forces of the will, then the feelings, then the intellect. Much of this takes the form of group work in which the children act out principles that they have learned. An example of this is taken from a biology lesson with class seven (12- and 13-year-olds):

The diagram on the board showed a simplified representation of red and blue blood flowing from the heart and through the lungs. The teacher began by splitting the class in halves, one of which represented the flow of the blood, and the other the flow of the air into and out of the lungs. The two groups moved in circles, but met and weaved in a figure of eight at one point, which represented the lungs. Once the children were able to do this they had to introduce clapping and stamping, the circle representing the blood using a faster rhythm (four to one) than that representing the breathing rate. The ultimate effect was almost hypnotic with the concentration and rhythm involved.

Blunt, 1999, p.176

This example illustrates one of the ways that scientific knowledge can be transformed into an artistic activity that creates much deeper understanding ("concrete concepts" in Piaget's terminology, or the "enactive mode of learning" in Bruner's). Involving large classes in such activities takes practice. The teacher needs to have authority within the class and to gradually build the skills and cooperation of the class towards the more complex movements.

Besides the usual forms of art, a specialized form of eurhythmy is practiced in which pupils learn to express the sounds of language through physical gesture. (Blunt, 1999). This creates an appreciation for the power of language. Maher and Bleach (1997) provide a rich selection of examples for the primary school and kindergarten of artistic activities designed to "put the heart back into teaching", which can be used with both large and small classes. A classic introductory text on the Waldorf tradition is Francis Edmund's book which attempts to explain to the modern mind the meaning of imaginative thinking; thinking imbued with feeling (Edmund, 1975).

## Conclusion

This outline of Waldorf principles has attempted to convey that it is not intended as a quick or easy answer to educational challenges. On the contrary, education through art demands sound training, imaginative planning and dedication. However, the principles make available a powerful approach to educating children from diverse backgrounds in contexts where more orthodox approaches fail. In addition, whereas, large classes in conventional schools threaten the effectiveness of teaching, large classes in Waldorf schools create greater opportunities for the principles to take effect, on condition that the teacher has established a sound relationship with each child in the class.

# References

Blunt, R.J.S. (1999). *Waldorf education: Theory and practice.* Cape Town, South Africa: Novalis Press.

Bruner, J.S. (1966). *Toward a theory of instruction.* Cambridge, MA: Belknap Press.

Drever, J. (1952). *A dictionary of psychology.* Harmondsworth, UK: Penguin Reference Books.

Edmund, F. (1975). *Rudolf Steiner's gift to education: The Waldorf Schools.* London: Rudolf Steiner Press.

Holt, J. (1972). *Freedom and beyond.* Harmondsworth, UK: Penguin.

Honey, P. and Mumford, A. (1982). *The manual of learning styles.* Maidenhead, UK: Peter Honey.

Kolb, D.A. (1976). *Learning style inventory.* Boston: McBer.

Maher, S. and Bleach, Y. (1997). *Putting the heart back into teaching: A manual for junior primary teachers* (2nd ed.). Cape Town, South Africa: Novalis Press.

Maher, S., & Shepherd, R. (1995). *Standing on the brink: An education for the 21st Century.* Cape Town, South Africa: Novalis Press.

Rogers, C. (1969). *Freedom to learn.* Charles E. Merrill Pub. Co.

Steiner, R. (1947). *The spiritual ground of education.* London: Anthroposophical Publishing Co.

Steiner, R. (1966). *Study of man.* Translated by D. Harwood and H. Fox, and revised by A.C. Harwood. London: Rudolf Steiner Press.

Steiner, R. (1967). *Discussions with teachers.* Translated by H. Fox. London: Rudolf Steiner Press.

Steiner, R. (1968). *The roots of education.* Translated by H. Fox. London: Rudolf Steiner Press.

Steiner, R. (1970). Education and the science of the spirit. Translated by M. Tapp and E. Tapp. In Allen, P.M. (Ed.). *Education as an art.* New York: Rudolf Steiner Publications.

Steiner, R. (1973). *Knowledge of the higher worlds. How is it achieved?* 6th Edition. Translated by D.S.O. and C.D. London: Rudolf Steiner Press.

Steiner, R. (1976). *Practical advice to teachers.* Translated by Johanna Collis. London: Rudolf Steiner Press.

# About the Author

**Richard Blunt**, D Ed, completed an analysis of Rudolf Steiner's educational thought and a case study of Waldorf Schools for his Master's thesis in education at Rhodes University, Grahamstown, South Africa. The thesis was later adapted for publication by Novalis

Press under the title *Waldorf Education: Theory and Practice*. The book is now in the bibliography of several training programmes for Waldorf teachers in South Africa, Australia and the United States. Richard Blunt went to school in Zambia and Zimbabwe. He began his teaching career as a remedial teacher, and then taught English as a first and second language at primary, secondary and university levels. He has also trained teachers at the Universities of Rhodes and Fort Hare, and is currently Director of Academic Development and Associate Professor in the Faculty of Education at the University of Port Elizabeth, South Africa. E-mail: indrjb@upe.ac.za.

# CHAPTER 5

# The Story of Two Schools in Israel

*Hanna Shachar*

Teachers everywhere complain about the large number of students in their classes. These complaints reflect reality prevailing in schools today (Sarason, 1990). Society in the post-industrial era has witnessed rapid population growth in urban centers, which naturally resulted in a parallel growth in the number of students in schools. Another feature of post-industrial society is the mobility of people between places of work and between countries. As a result, many classrooms in different countries have become highly heterogeneous, culturally and linguistically (Oakes, 1985; Landis & Bahagat, 1996).

During the past 4 decades, expectations of schools for transmitting knowledge and even for solving social problems have risen (Goodlad, 1984; Sarason, 1983, 1996). There is widespread recognition of the difficulties that schools experience in coping with large numbers of students. These large school populations have generated, inter alia, considerable alienation and violent behavior (Sarason, 2001) as well as dissatisfaction with students' academic achievement. These conditions have led to wave after wave of educational reforms and programs of school change (Conley, 1997; Dalin & Rolf, 1993; Darling-Hammond, 1997; Deal & Petterson, 1990; Joyce, Wolf & Calhoun, 1993). However, initiatives for changing schools have had little effect on the preparation of teachers. Close examination of teacher education programs in many institutions of higher learning reveals outdated approaches that do not provide teaching candidates with appropriate competencies for functioning in today's schools (Goodlad, Soder & Sirotnik, 1990; Wideen, Mayer-Smith & Moon, 1998). Recently, new ideas about the training of future teachers have been suggested (Cohen, Brody, Davidson, & Sapon-Shevin, in press) but they are seldom implemented in institutions that prepare prospective teachers.

One of the more creative suggestions intended to overcome the discontinuity between the reality in schools and the preparation of educators was to transform the school itself into a learning organization (Putnam & Borko, 2000; Senge, 1990), and/or into what is known as professional development schools (Lieberman, 1988). In this kind of setting, the teaching staff of a school engages in investigating its own conceptions and goals to ascertain the proper means needed to implement them (Shachar, 1996).

## Pedagogical and Organizational Changes in Schools

According to Bennette (1996), it is no longer a matter for debate that large classes harm students and impose difficulties on teachers. It should be mentioned, however, that this statement applies almost exclusively to the traditional manner of classroom teaching and learning. I refer to the school organized in such a way that a teacher teaches a specific subject to four or five classes a day, and that he or she is constrained to transmit to the students a given quantity of academic material on which they will be tested. Undoubtedly, such conditions impose serious limitations on teachers' effectiveness. Moreover, teachers' effectiveness will decline more as the class increases in size. This state of affairs exhausts teachers, physically and emotionally, and is detrimental to students, particularly to those who need added attention and guidance (Shachar & Eitan, in press). It should be recalled that such conditions are not dictated by some *force majeur*. Reliable research and educational theory during the past 3 decades show clearly that these conditions can be changed (Conley, 1997; Fullan, 1993; Sharan, Shachar & Levin, 1999).

It has become clear that a strong relationship exists between patterns of school organization and limiting classroom size. More specifically, the relationship is between school organization and the ratio of the number of students to the number of teachers who teach them at any given time (Carroll, 1990, 1994; Sizer, 1984, 1993). For example, a school can decide that the process of student learning need not necessarily be limited to the area within the school walls. Students can engage in learning, in part at least, in other community settings including museums, industries, public services and so forth (Sarason & Lorentz, 1979; Raywid, 1995). As a result of such a decision, people associated with these settings contribute to students' education in addition to their teachers. Moreover, this style of learning radically alters the traditional form of instruction, with students selecting both the location and the topic of their study. Teachers might be called upon to serve as advisors to small groups of students who select the same topic for study. A decision of that kind by the school faculty involves considerable change in the entire manner of the school's operation and organization. A school staff may not possess the knowledge needed for a change of this kind and a transition to this manner of organizing student learning will probably require the advice of various consultants. In this fashion, schools can become transformed into learning organizations.

The present chapter relates events that occurred in two schools where teachers and principals changed the patterns of instruction and organization of time to make instruction more efficient. One consequence of this change was that any single teacher taught fewer students at a given time, and relationships between teachers and students improved, as did student learning.

*The two schools described here enjoyed little if any increase in resources or in the number of teachers assigned to the school. Nevertheless, the pedagogical changes introduced improved considerably the nature of the relationship between teachers and students. These kinds of changes are essential to the quality of life in schools for students and for teachers.*

## The Gordon Junior-High School

Almost 1,000 students populated grades 7 to 9 in this school with 40 per class. The teaching staff consisted of more than 50 teachers, most of whom had many years experience as teachers and in this school. A total of 25 teachers were responsible for specific classrooms and the rest were part-time teachers for art, music, health, special education and so on. In 1993, the principal retired and a new one was appointed. As part of her effort to become acquainted with the teaching staff, the principal gradually understood that the teachers were generally satisfied with conditions as they were and did not express any expectations for change. A year later the principal undertook to cultivate a team of pedagogical leaders. Teachers who perceived themselves to be potential leaders in the school were asked to participate in a workshop with the school's administration and supervisor. The purpose of the workshop was to engage in a cooperative effort to clarify a number of pedagogical issues such as how the school conceived of its ideal graduate, the roles of subject matter coordinators, the nature of teacher-student relationships, how staff members can/should cooperate with one another, and so forth. The group continued to meet over the course of the year. At the end of the year, 20 teachers were, in the principal's words, "far less satisfied with existing conditions in the school than they had been previously." Members of this group conducted a series of discussions with other members of the faculty directed at improving the school.

The following academic year was devoted to defining and specifying the school's educational outlook. Each teacher who had been a member of the original workshop team chaired a workshop for other teachers. At the end of that year an educational and social policy was formulated and a document presenting this new conception was prepared. The document highlighted the gap between the school's proclaimed intentions and its actual performance.

Many teachers agreed that the first step was to implement the new conception by strengthening the relationship between teachers and their students. Everyone considered that relationship to be the basic foundation of the educational process, without which no improvement in school functioning could be achieved. One thing was certain—time was needed for personal contact between teachers and students. The teachers claimed that class size had to be reduced and the perpetual pursuit of "coverage" of academic material at a rapid pace had to be replaced with a different kind of relationship between teachers and students.

A steering committee was set up to work out a comprehensive plan of school change. The committee consulted with the district supervisor, the teachers' union, the local municipal government, students and parents. The final plan was presented to all the groups mentioned above, as well as to the Ministry of Education for final approval.

***Description of the Project***   The teachers' operational plan began by listing these basic principles:

1. School is part of life and not merely preparation for life (Dewey, 1938).

2.  Learning occurs all the time and everywhere. School must preserve students' curiosity and provide them with a variety of learning skills.
3.  The school views itself as part of the community. Therefore, many sites in the community are appropriate for learning. This notion dramatically expands the school's pool of resources for enriching students' learning.
4.  The roles of teachers and students will change. Teachers will serve as guides and consultants to students and assist them to assume responsibility for their own learning.
5.  Groups of students engaged in learning need not necessarily be composed on the basis of age. Cross-age grouping can foster cooperation and mutual assistance among students.
6.  Students should participate in planning their studies to raise their level of motivation.
7.  The teaching staff affirms the role of the school in developing students' sense of responsibility towards the community. Each student should devote a set amount of time to a community work/study project.
8.  Students' learning activities in school should be more varied and not restricted to the accepted disciplines coupled with the typical examination. Students should be encouraged to succeed in new domains of knowledge and to cultivate different abilities. It should be possible for a maximum number of students to experience success and develop a positive self-image.
9.  Students should participate in multiple settings such as small groups, project teams, committees, workshops, community projects and so forth. The goal is to foster communication with many people of different ages.

It is important to remember that this systematic development of these principles occupied 3 years of cooperative teamwork. At the conclusion of this period most teachers had a clear understanding of the school's goals. Teachers said that these principles constituted a breakthrough in their professional thinking. The principles listed above were given the following operational formulation:

1.  Students will select a community site where they will work as part of their personal study schedule (The school provided a list of 22 possible sites).

2. Students will work in multi-age groups at the site they chose, each group with 10 to 15 members. Each week the groups' work will alternate between morning and afternoon.
3. The scope of study of school subjects should be broadened by visits to sites outside the school which are nevertheless related to topics under study in the school. Such visits will be conducted once in 2 weeks.
4. One day a week will be devoted to discussions of current events. The school will conduct a select number of workshops and discussions, and students will choose the ones in which they are interested.
5. A significant portion of school learning will be accomplished through research by students working in groups or as individuals, and counseled by teachers. Therefore, teachers must function for part of their time in school as guides and consultants to the students.

In order to carry out these operational plans, the principal and the steering committee decided on the following changes. First, all the academic hours normally devoted to art, music, home economics, technology and computers would be exchanged for providing consultation and guidance for groups of students engaged in projects they chose to carry out in various community settings. Teachers of the above subjects would function as facilitators for the students in regard to their research work. Second, after the plan was submitted to the Ministry of Education for approval, the school was granted 8 hours a week of extra time, and, in turn, the school distributed these paid hours among 8 special subject teachers (not homeroom teachers) who did not receive any supplementary salary. On their part, these

*Teachers learned the theoretical and practical difference between traditional whole-class instruction where a teacher is the sole decision maker and evaluator and the role of guiding students in research work where students choose the topic and are responsible for implementing their investigation. This change was not easy for the teachers.*

teachers joined the staff of teachers available for offering assistance to student research/work groups.

Third, instead of working in the community, 9th-grade students could choose to serve as tutors for 7th graders working with computers. In this way, some teachers who taught computer courses were freed from classroom teaching hours, and their time was also added to the pool of teachers available for assisting students' work in small groups.

Two problems arose immediately after the decision about these procedures was made. One was that the teachers had no preparation for working in the role of guides to groups of 20 students. The second problem was the need for replanning the school's schedule. An in-service training course for the teachers was conducted. Teachers learned the theoretical and practical difference between traditional whole-class instruction where a teacher is the sole decision maker and evaluator and the role of guiding students in research work where students choose the topic and are responsible for implementing their investigation. This change was not easy for the teachers. Out of a group of 32 teachers who took part in the in-service training and worked for a year in their new role, 5 decided not to continue. The other teachers repeatedly indicated that it took them a long time to overcome their old patterns of work and function in new ways (Sarason, 1990).

The need for replanning the school schedule stemmed directly from the fact that it would be impossible to carry out the new ideas that the teachers had formulated while maintaining the traditional allocation of teachers to subjects and classrooms. After many consultations with the district supervisor and the local board of education, it was decided to divide the school into "houses", each with its own teaching staff and student body (Sizer, 1984). In each house, the teachers and students assumed collective responsibility for their work. Each teacher became responsible for 25 students without regard for his or her subject of specialization. All teachers without exception were included in this program.

***Learning and Volunteer Work in Community Settings*** The school set up relationships with 22 community institutions including clubs for senior citizens, special education kindergartens, museums, commercial organizations, fire fighting units and so forth. As noted, the plan was for students to work in these settings in small groups according to their choice. The people in charge of the various settings would be responsible for assigning tasks to the student groups. One teacher accompanied each group. During the course of the year, students selected a topic for study related to the setting where they did their volunteer work. The students were advised by teachers about how to prepare a written report on their work and how to use various methods for gathering information, such as observations, interviews, and preparing models. Students learned to choose the research method appropriate to their topic.

As a result of all these activities, a typical student's week in school assumed a completely different character from what it was in the past. Students were located outside the school for 10% of the school week. An additional 25% of the time was spent in groups of 10 to 20 led by 1 teacher. The remaining 65% of the school week was devoted to regular classroom study.

At the end of the first year of volunteer work in the community, the school conducted a survey in order to learn about the students' perceptions of their experience. The results showed that the relationships that were established between the teachers and the students in the small groups had a significant effect on students' satisfaction with their work in the community settings. Results also showed that the younger students (Grade 7) were significantly more satisfied from the change in the school's traditional learning patterns than were students from Grade 9.

Students stressed the satisfaction they derived from working in small groups. One teacher responsible for the volunteer work in the community interviewed 5 teachers and 17 students whom she chose at random. She inquired about their perceptions of the teacher-student relationships upon conclusion of the academic year. Teachers noted that students began to talk about themselves more openly and more trust and respect were established between students and teachers. A phrase that arose often in the interviews was "there is a relaxed atmosphere and the work is being performed whole-heartedly." Some teachers remarked that there was a "pleasant and positive climate" in the groups, no competition and much mutual assistance and cooperation. The most obvious result of this evaluation was that both teachers and students noted the warm and close relationships that were formed between teachers and students.

It appears that at the end of the year during which students worked in these informal groups with the teachers, the initial difficulties did not prevent teachers and students from responding very positively to this experience.

***Summary*** The school underwent changes that impacted on all its domains of operation including class schedules, teachers' roles, patterns of student learning, and, of course, the school's relation to the community. As a result, almost all interactions among school personnel and students, as well as between people in and outside of the school (including parents) were affected significantly.

1. Teachers noted that their work with the students in the community and the many tours of community sites taken together gave teachers the opportunity to learn about many aspects of their students that otherwise they would not have known.

   Students reacted to these experiences by manifesting a much higher level of motivation to attend school (absentee rates declined dramatically) and with a distinctly higher level of trust in their teachers. During any given week, students spent 12 hours as members of groups of 20 or less, although there were still many classes with the usual 40 students (a typical week consisted of 36 hours of class time). Teachers agreed that the experience of belonging to a research team working in the community exerted considerable influence on the climate prevailing in the larger classes, and that the verbal communication in the latter classes between teachers and students was far less formal, more subject oriented and generally more open than previously (Hertz-Lazarowtiz & Shachar, 1990).

2. Students met many people in the community who contributed to their learning experiences. Consultation with the teachers assisted students to derive maximum benefit from their meetings with people in the community. The students understood these encounters more clearly after group discussions.

3. During one of the meetings of the steering committee that included representatives of the local board of education, the district supervisor and parents, 9th graders commented on the positive change apparent in their classmates' behavior toward students in lower grades. The seventh graders, on their part, stated that by contrast with earlier days, they no longer hesitated to mingle with the older students in the hallways.

4. The change in the school succeeded in involving many parents who assisted their children engaged in projects conducted in retirement homes, the municipal storage center for emergency

equipment, and so forth. Parents' interest in the school grew considerably.

Even without an administrative change in the number of students or teachers in the school that could reduce the size of the classrooms, the teachers' "load" of students in the classes was reduced. This was due to the change in pedagogical and organizational conceptions of the school staff, coupled with the fact that the school learned how to plan and receive support for its change from the local authorities (including the teachers' union). This school's experience shows that the organization of alternative teaching styles that increase the quality of teachers' contact with students in situations outside the formal environment of the classroom affects the entire ecology of the school and, in turn, positively affects classroom learning. The nature of the relationships between students and teachers in the classroom changed markedly as a result of their collaboration outside the school where they were not subject to the constraints of teaching-by-lecture during a 45-minute period. Another conclusion that can be reached from this experience is that the teacher-student ratio can be reduced almost without increasing the resources of the school. This can be accomplished by a different distribution of staff personnel with different sized groups of students, along with a parallel change in the school's schedule of classes.

## Mt. Hermon High School

This senior high school in Israel has 700 students in grades 9 to 12, with 60 teachers and other staff members. Graduates of the school usually take the national examinations in Israel administered over the course of several years before graduation. The school has been in operation for more than 45 years, and its teaching staff is stable with above average seniority. In recent years, the number of graduates taking the national examinations declined, as has the average score of those who did take the test. Obviously, this state of affairs caused dissatisfaction among members of the staff.

A process of school change was initiated in 1995 with an in-service course for all principals and vice principals in this particular town, in which the principal and vice principal of Mt. Hermon School participated. The workshop stressed the following topics:

1. Alternative styles of school organization, contrasting a social-systems approach to the typical bureaucratic–hierarchical model;

2. A process of survey-feedback to identify school problems in need of attention;
3. Skills for conducting a systematic approach to team problem solving and decision-making;
4. The theoretical background of team decision-making; and
5. Cooperative learning methods, particularly Jigsaw and Group Investigation (Sharan, 1999) and how principals can assist teachers to implement these methods in classrooms.

In the workshop on the survey-feedback method, participants listed the problems in their schools about which information was needed in order to understand them more fully, and to be in a better position to cope with them. The principal of Mt. Hermon High School mentioned low student motivation as one of the chief problems that concerned him. During the course of the workshop, the principal and vice principal of that school prepared—with input from 6 teachers—a questionnaire to assess the level of student motivation to learn. After collecting the data from the students, the principal convened a teachers' meeting where he presented the findings of the survey, following which the teachers were divided into small groups to analyze the students' responses to the questionnaire. Each group was also asked to suggest solutions to the problems reflected in the findings. Results supported the principal's contention that students in the school expressed a low level of motivation to learn to the point where many students revealed a lack of interest in continuing any kind of education after graduation from high school.

Teachers in the school discussed the results obtained from students' responses to the questionnaire. Most of the teachers admitted that the teaching methods currently used in the school were outdated, boring and unable to meet the students' needs. Most of the suggestions offered by the groups of teachers focused on the urgent need to acquire new instructional methods and to change the nature of teaching in the school.

***Preparation for Change***   The school's administration decided to set up two teams of 13 teachers per team: one to study the subject of "improving motivation" and the other to study "improving achievement". The team dealing with the latter topic was to assess students' grades on the national examinations and to reach some conclusions about the reasons for the recent decline in their scores. After intense study, consultations and discussions, the "motivation" team concluded that there was no direct approach to improving student motivation to learn. Instructional methods and the structure of the curriculum would have to be changed in order to raise motivation. The teams functioned for close to half of the academic year.

Following this work, the principal decided to initiate an experiment to decrease the number of subjects studied by students at any given time. Two or more disciplines could be combined into one "cluster" of subjects to be studied in an integrated fashion, and students would investigate this "trans-disciplinary domain" by use of the Group Investigation method of cooperative learning (Sharan, Shachar and Levine, 1999; Sharan and Sharan, 1992). An in-service project was planned and carried out in which the principal and 12 teachers designated to teach 9th grade took part. The in-service course concentrated on two topics: (i) teaching an integrated trans-disciplinary curriculum and (ii) the Group Investigation method. The principal kept all teachers in the school informed of steps taken and plans for the future.

After 4 months of workshops (twice a month for 2½ hour meetings) the senior staff began to plan the change in the school schedule required by the new instructional and curricular approaches. The plan encompassed 7 regular 9th-grade classes although a 9th-grade class of "slow learners" was not included temporarily.

The teaching staff was asked to decide what kinds of curricular "clusters' it wished to identify among all the subjects taught in the school, and with whom each teacher wished to work as a team when teaching a given cluster. Each teacher who had participated in the workshops interviewed one or two teachers who had not participated but who were scheduled to be included in the experiment with the 9th grade during the next academic year. They were invited to express their preferences for the formation of clusters. The interviews also aimed at giving all the teachers a sense of inclusion in the project and a feeling that decisions were not made without their knowledge. They were asked to what extent they agreed to have disciplines combined in an integrated way, how prepared they were to teach in a program of that kind, and what class size would be best for this plan. Interview results showed that 72% of the teachers expressed willingness to try out the new approach, while 28% had many doubts and hesitations.

Although teachers expressed their willingness to take part in this project, they indicated that classes should be composed of fewer students than the usual (36 to 40). It appears that teachers who agree to try a new method feel more confident when the class is smaller than usual. The administration of the school was surprised to learn that only 21% of the teachers wanted to retain the accepted method of testing students as the mode of evaluation. The majority of the teachers wanted to adopt methods of evaluation more in tune with the suggested change in instructional method.

*The Change Plan*   The teaching staff decided to establish five transdisciplinary clusters that encompassed twelve separate disciplines. However, after consultation with the district supervisor and officials, the decision was made to limit the scope of the project to three clusters encompassing six subject areas that will be taught cooperatively for two quarters (12 weeks) by a team of teachers. Even in its more limited conception, the plan underwent several transformations as it passed through the hands of different readers, including the teams scheduled to teach the clusters, until it reached its final formulation. The final plan included the following topics:

1. Israel's water problem. Conservation of water from natural sources and the effects of water (or its scarcity) on people, as these topics appear in the study of Biology and Chemistry. These subject teachers would work as a team renamed The Science Team.
2. Leaders and leadership. The subjects represented in this cluster were Literature and Bible, and these subject teachers would constitute the team.
3. Development towns in Israel during the 1950s. The teachers of History and Sociology undertook to teach this cluster.

The basic guidelines for teaching the clusters were: (i) the academic year would be divided into quarters or two semesters each with two quarters depending upon needs as they arise; (ii) each cluster would be taught daily or at least 3 times a week; (iii) each class session would be 90 or 120 minutes, as needed; (iv) a team of at least 2 teachers would conduct the classes; (v) the Group Investigation method would be used; and (vi) evaluation of student achievement would be based on the nature of the instruction.

The experiment required a significant change in the school's schedule, as well as coordination between the teams and the library, science labs and other facilities in the school. It turned out that students could consult any 3 adults in a given class about their research work. The class schedule made it possible for a small group of 4 to 5 students to have continuous and uninterrupted time to meaningfully progress in their work (Carroll, 1994). Time was also allocated for the teaching teams to meet and plan how they would cooperate in carrying out their work. The new schedule called for a weekly round of eight 2-hour classes, i.e. 16 hours of class work, which constituted half of a student's total class hours per week. For each of the two classrooms (80 students) there were two subject-matter teachers, a librarian, and a computer teacher. As noted, an additional element was the time set aside for planning by teams that were to teach the various clusters. Classes for physical education, Arabic language and music were concentrated on a single day, thereby releasing the cluster teams for a 3-hour meeting devoted to planning.

*Preparing Special-subject Teachers*   Once the senior staff of the school prepared the plan for the experiment, it was necessary to begin in-service training for the teachers. During the 2-month summer vacation that preceded the beginning of the experiment, as well as during the first two months of the new academic year, teachers of six subjects were grouped into three clusters. A total of 20 teachers took part in a series of workshops on the Group Investigation method. Topics studied in the workshops included developing students' discussion skills, locating sources of information to deal with problems under study, methods of alternative evaluation of individuals and groups, problems that might arise during conduct of the experiment, demonstration and examples of teaching trans-disciplinary curricular topics, and planning the first month of the experiment.

As the theory and procedures of Group Investigation appear in several publications, only an outline is presented here. Student groups progress through a series of six stages: (i) planning broad topics of study; (ii) planning the means needed to investigate those topics or problems; (iii) implementation of the group's plan; (iv) planning and preparation of a collective group product; (v) presentation of the group's product in a variety of ways; and (vi) evaluation of the entire process and product of the group's work by students and teacher (Sharan and Sharan, 1992, 1999).

To help them with planning the various stages of implementing Group Investigation, the teachers received specially-prepared checklists (such as, a checklist of questions for the organization stage and a checklist of questions for the research stage). Teachers planned their lessons cooperatively, discussing the questions raised using the checklists for each stage of the project. The project consultant met with each team of teachers for a month, after the workshops and before the experiment at the start of the new academic year, to summarize all the details. A meeting of all teams was held a week before the school year began to evaluate the progress of the experiment, and coordinate final details of the implementation. Teachers decided to make an announcement about the experiment to the entire school to give the students a boost in morale and to let them know that an important change was taking place.

**Implementing the Experiment**   In November, 2 months after the beginning of the academic year, the experiment began and lasted approximately 2 months. The 1st week was devoted entirely to presenting the new approach of teaching and learning to the students, although they had been informed about it since the start of the year. The students were eager to begin. The experiment progressed as students did research on the topics they chose, as part of the general subject announced by the teachers. Students displayed a great deal of enthusiasm for the project in general, and during the preparation of their presentations or exhibitions in particular. Their ideas for exhibiting what they had investigated were original and varied, including the preparation of TV programs, computer presentations of different kinds, videotapes and so forth.

   The following are examples of multidisciplinary topics that students chose. The group that studied Israel's water problems decided to deal with the factors that damage the aquifers, such as industrial waste, and with the means available for maintaining the ecological balance necessary for safeguarding Israel's natural reserves of drinking water. The biology teacher served as the advisor to this group. A second group concentrated on the short and long term effects on people of the chlorination of drinking water. The

*The number of students actively involved in learning increased dramatically. Without doubt, the new model of instruction, curricular organization into clusters, team teaching and the new schedule of classes, all contributed to a significant improvement in student motivation to learn.*

chemistry teacher advised this group. Teachers of literature and Bible worked in a similar fashion on the general topic of leaders and leadership. Groups of students chose famous leaders beginning in biblical times up to figures appearing in recent works of literature. Each group analyzed one figure from various points of view. They consulted with the history teacher or literature teacher as required by the subject at hand. All the groups completed their work with presentations to the class and evaluations of their work.

*Teachers' Reactions*  At the end of the two quarters during which the experiment was conducted, a meeting of all the teachers involved was held to summarize what had happened. Some teachers analyzed events with an aim to pointing out features that succeeded well and others that needed to be changed or improved. An example of a technical problem was that the teacher responsible for the library was inadequately prepared for assisting students in their projects, and the criteria for evaluating students' products were not clear. An example of success was the increase in students' ratings of lessons. Many previously passive students became involved in learning activities, giving teachers a sense of satisfaction.

The difficulties raised by the teachers are typical when schools implement new projects with which teachers are unfamiliar, and when they are exposed more pointedly to the gap between what teachers may have learned or consider to be desirable, and what they encounter in reality (Wideen, Mayer-Smith & Moon, 1998). It is also important to recall that this experiment was limited to the 9th grade, while teachers and students in the 10th through 12th grades continued to function using the traditional model of teaching and of school organization. On occasion, the presence of two different models of organization led to temporary unpleasant misunderstanding between teachers. In the new cluster model, for example where students engaged in investigating topics, they frequently had to leave the classroom to go to the library, to a lab or elsewhere to locate the information they needed. Yet, the traditional model of schooling had a teacher on patrol to prevent students from milling around in the hallways during class time. Once, a teacher on hall duty stopped students who appeared in the hall on their way to the library and reprimanded them for not being in their classroom. That caused the students considerable confusion and unpleasantness until the teacher from the cluster arrived and explained why the students were in the hall.

In light of experiences of this kind, teachers suggested that the school as a whole should adopt the new model so there could be a higher level of coordination and continuity in the policy and organization of the school. This and other recommendations that emerged from the meeting promised to contribute to an improved level of implementation at the next stage of this project.

*Summary*   The teachers formulated the most important results that emerged from this experiment. The number of students actively involved in learning increased dramatically. It should be recalled that the fundamental problem that fueled the entire undertaking was the low level of student motivation to learn, clearly documented by a survey-feedback project initiated by the principal. Without doubt, the new model of instruction, curricular organization into clusters, team teaching and the new schedule of classes, all contributed to a significant improvement in student motivation to learn. One student remarked, "We discovered that the teachers can be our friends and help us." Another said," The teacher was not just a source of information but also a guide and counselor, and that's how we learned to ask questions and look for answers."

The experimental project created conditions whereby 1 teacher was responsible for 20 to 25 students for approximately half the number of hours that a student ordinarily attended class during a given week. For every two classes of 80 students there were 2 teachers to teach the cluster of two disciplines, plus the librarian and the teacher of computers. In addition, the change in the method of teaching and learning that made it possible for students to choose topics of study as members of small groups engaged in doing research on those topics, completely altered the dynamics of the relationships between students and teachers. Prior to the experiment, the school had its share of behavior and discipline problems for which teachers were constantly seeking solutions. In the 9th-grade classes where the experiment was conducted, behavior problems declined radically. Everyone, teachers and students alike, said that these classes had a much more relaxed atmosphere than the traditionally taught classes.

## Conclusion

The two schools described here enjoyed little if any increase in resources or in the number of teachers assigned to the school. Nevertheless, the pedagogical changes introduced, such as using community settings as sites for learning or the introduction of team teaching of "clusters" of subject matter, led to the reduction in the number of students that teachers met for instruction during the course of any given week, and also improved considerably the nature of the relationship between teachers and students. These kinds of changes are essential to the quality of life in schools for students and for teachers. These changes are consistent with the best of educational theory and practice that has emerged in recent decades.

## References

Bennett, N. (1996). Class size in primary schools: Perceptions of headmasters, chairs of governors, teachers and parents. *British Educational Research Journal, 22*, 33-55.

Carroll, J. (1990). The Copernican plan: Restructuring the American high school. *Phi Delta Kappan, 71*, 358-365.

Carroll, J. (1994). The Copernican plan evaluated: The evaluation of a revolution. *Phi Delta Kappan, 76*, 105-113.

Cohen, E., Brody, C., Davidson, N., & Sapon-Shevin, M. (Eds.)(in press). *Cooperative learning for future teachers: Teacher educators pave the way.* New York: Teachers College Press.

Conley, D. (1997). *Mapping school restructuring.* ERIK publications.

Dalin, P., & Rolf, H. (1993). *Changing the school culture.* London: Cassell.

Darling-Hammond, L. (1997). *The right to learn: A blue print for creating schools that work.* San Francisco: Jossey-Bass.

Deal, T., & Petterson, K. (1990). *The principal's role in shaping school culture.* Washington, DC: US Department of Education.

Dewey, J. (1938). *Experience and education.* New York: McMillan.

Hertz-Lazarowitz, R., & Shahchar, H. (1990). Teachers' verbal behavior in cooperative and whole-class instruction. In S. Sharan (Ed.), *Cooperative learning: Theory and research.* New York: Praeger

Fullan, M. (1993). *Change forces.* London: Cassell.

Goodlad, J. (1984). *A place called school.* New York: McGraw Hill.

Goodlad, J., Soder, R., & Sirotnik, K. (1990). *Places where teachers are taught.* San Francisco: Jossey-Bass.

Joyce, B., Wolf, J., & Calhoun, E. (1993). *The self renewing school.* Alexandria, VA: Association for Supervision and Curriculum Development.

Landis, D., & Bahagat, R. (Eds.) (1996). *Handbook of intercultural training* (2nd ed.). Thousand Oaks, CA: Sage.

Lieberman, A. (1988). *Building a professional culture in schools.* New York: Teachers College Press.

Oakes, J. (1985). *Keeping track: How schools structure inequality.* New Haven, CT: Yale University Press.

Putnam, R., & Borko, H. (2000). What do new views of knowledge and thinking have to say about research on teacher learning? *Educational Researcher, 29* (1), 4-15.

Raywid, M. (1995). Professional community and its yield at Metro Academy. In K. Louis and D. Kruse (Eds.), *Professionalism and community: Perspectives on reforming urban schools.* Thousand Oaks, CA: Corwin Press.

Sarason, S. (1983). *Schooling in America: Scapegoat and salvation.* New York: Free Press.

Sarason, S. (1990). *The predictable failure of educational reform.* San Francisco: Jossey-Bass.

Sarason, S. (1996). *Revisiting "the culture of school and the problem of change".* New York: Teachers College Press.

Sarason, S. (2001). *American psychology & schools: A critique.* New York: Teachers College Press.

Sarason, S., & Lorentz, E. (1979). *The challenge of the resource exchange network.* San Francisco: Jossey-Bass.

Senge, P. (1990). *The fifth discipline: The art and practice of the learning organization.* New York: Doubleday.

Shachar, H. (1996). Developing new traditions in secondary schools: A working model for organizational and instructional change. *Teachers College Record, 97*(4), 549-568.

Shachar, H., & Eitan, T. (in press). *Group investigation and the quantity of students' writing in heterogeneous junior-high school classrooms.*

Sharan, S. (1999) (Ed.). *Handbook of cooperative learning methods* (2nd ed.). Westport, CT: Praeger.

Sharan, S., Shachar, H., & Levin, T. (1999). *The innovative school: Organization and instruction.* Westport, CT: Bergin & Garvey.

Sharan, Y., & Sharan, S. (1992). *Expanding cooperative learning through group investigation.* New York: Teachers College Press.

Sharan, Y., & Sharan, S. (1999). Group investigation in the cooperative classroom. In S. Sharan (Ed.) *Handbook of cooperative learning methods* (2nd ed.). Westport, CT: Praeger.

Sizer, T. (1984). *Horace's compromise: The dilemma of the American high school.* Boston: Houghton-Mifflin.

Sizer, T. (1993) *Horace's school: Redesigning the American high school.* Boston: Houghton-Mifflin.

Wideen, M., Mayer-Smith, J., & Moon, B. (1998). A critical analysis of the research on learning to teach: Making the case for an ecological perspective on inquiry. *Review of Educational Research, 68* (2), 130-178.

## About the Author

**Hanna Shachar,** Ph D, is a senior lecturer in the School of Education at Bar-Ilan University, Ramat Gan, Israel. She directed citywide projects to introduce participative management in school organization and cooperative learning in classroom instruction. Her international experience includes working with the National Board of Education in Helsinki, Finland, and teacher training for cooperative learning in Singapore. She is co-author with Shlomo Sharan and Tamar Levin of *The Innovative School: Organization and Instruction* (1999), and was a guest editor with Shlomo Sharan and George Jacobs of *Asia Pacific Journal of Education*: Special Issue on Cooperative Learning (2002). E-mail: hannashachar@hotmail.com

# CHAPTER 6

# Incorporating Indigenous Knowledge in Post-secondary Teaching

*Jessica Ball*

This chapter describes a 'generative curriculum' approach that: (a) promotes active learning by encouraging students to participate in the construction of knowledge; and (b) ensures the relevance of curriculum by asking learners to investigate topics that arise from local social development goals. Three pilot projects, spanning two decades and three continents, are described here to illustrate this generative approach. All involve post-secondary training in areas of social science or human services. Rather than defining the relevant content of the curriculum in advance of the course, the pilot projects demonstrate a process-oriented, 'generative' approach: only part of the curriculum is pre-scripted and part of it evolves during the course through students' interactions among themselves and with representatives of their cultural communities.

*A key principle guiding the three pilot projects is that effective education begins with acceptance of a desire on the part of students to participate in iden-tifying at least some of the content, choosing at least some of the activities, and participating in at least some of the assessment of their own learning.*

The projects are presented in the chapter in chronological order. The first project, located in Malaysia, is described briefly to introduce principles that have been substantially expanded in the latter two innovations involving my colleague, Alan Pence, at the University of Victoria, Canada, and myself. The first project represented my first significant movement away from a didactic approach to a student- and community-centered approach that involved non-student community members and elevated the importance of indigenous knowledge. The second project, involving indigenous communities in Canada, is ongoing and has clearly demonstrated the benefits to students and communities of opening up the foundations of curriculum and teaching so that education is culturally sustaining and grounded in community development. The third case, located in sub-Saharan Africa, offers a preview of a project that will explore the principles of 'generative' curriculum with a networked cohort of learners whose interactions include technologically mediated discussion, face-to-face group work and community consultation.

The driving force for all of the projects is the hope of most communities and countries that education will make sense (that is, resonate with and be useful) to students and the local communities where they are expected to be of service.

> Having taught mainstream courses in two different colleges, I can say that doing the Generative Curriculum, where people representing the students' own cultures play a big role in the teaching, is wonderful. It's so engaging for the students to have that connection to their community right in the curriculum, and it increases their self-esteem to have their culture valued in that way. It gives the program that they're taking credibility, because they know that what they're learning is going to be relevant and it isn't just a canned curriculum brought in from somewhere else. When you're doing mainstream kind of teaching, it's that old approach of filling an empty vessel, and this level of meaning and credibility just doesn't tend to happen.
>
> Instructor, Cowichan Partnership Program, Canada

A primary purpose of post-secondary education is to promote active exploration and experimentation with new ways of knowing, new criteria for analyzing, evaluating, and combining knowledge and innovative practice models. Yet, a persistent challenge for educators is the question of how to move substantially beyond teacher-directed transmission models, in which learners are passive and learning outcomes are limited, to learners' wholesale adoption of pre-conceived paradigms for producing, organizing and applying knowledge. Educators continue to struggle to find ways to promote creative, critical thinking and to remove barriers to inclusion of non-traditional knowledge sources, including 'indigenous' knowledge. Since everyone is indigenous to somewhere and therefore all knowledge is indigenous with reference to some location, 'indigenous knowledge' for purposes of the present discussion is defined as knowledge that is embedded in a local geo-cultural community, that has evolved over a long period within that setting, and that is not knowingly imported from a 'foreign' geo-cultural context.

## Incorporating Indigenous Knowledge in Teaching and Learning

Post-secondary education reflects and engenders the culturally conditioned values and practices of those who design and deliver the curricula. This is especially evident in social science, teacher training, and other human service training. Many educators around the globe, especially outside of North America, have expressed concern about the lack of representation of non-Western values, content, and methods at all levels of education (Smith, 1999; Battiste & Barman, 1995; Ki-Zerbo, Kane, Archibald, Lizop, & Rahnema, 1997). There is growing concern among some observers of 'international' education and exchange projects in the majority, non-Western world about the harm that can and has been done by ethnocentric curriculum, programs of research and technical assistance presided over by Western educators (Ball, 1998; Dahlberg, Moss, & Pence, 1999; Ki-Zerbo, Kane, Archibald, Lizop, & Rahnema,1997; Shiva, 1997). This critique extends to the well-documented experience of cultural holocaust caused by the imposition of 'best practices' in Western education on traditional cultures, languages and communities of indigenous peoples in North America (Battiste & Barman, 1995). A concern with promoting an anti-colonial approach to education was a major impetus for my involvement in the three pilot projects described in this chapter.

## Participatory Teaching and Learning

A key principle guiding the three pilot projects is that effective education begins with acceptance of a desire on the part of students to participate in identifying at least some of the content, choosing at least some of the activities, and participating in at least some of the assessment of their own learning. We have learned from research the importance of student-centered teaching strategies that promote 'active learning' rather than passive receipt of provided knowledge at all levels (Ball, 1994). For most students, true engagement in learning requires a curriculum that is relevant and personally meaningful and that affirms the student's own identity and experiences, as well as classroom processes that empower students, giving them a sense of self-direction and self-efficacy (Freire, 1993; Giroux, 1992; Lockhart, 1982). These conclusions have been reinforced in my research evaluating the pilot project with indigenous peoples of Canada (Ball, 2001). A participatory approach is essential within an anti-colonial agenda.

## Teaching as if Students and Communities Mattered

In the three pilot projects described in this chapter, students, their communities, and institutional supporters have sought education that encompasses both locally generated knowledge and knowledge from established canons in Western academe. In the words of an indigenous educator involved in the pilot project in Canada: "We wanted to give students the best of both worlds, and enable them to walk in both worlds." All three pilot projects enable graduates to work in their local communities in ways that sustain and revitalize local cultures. At the same time, graduates acquire credentials and knowledge that have enabled them to develop careers beyond the local setting.

*The effectiveness of this approach would seem to depend less upon the size of the class, and more upon the instructor. The instructor needs to be comfortable with not knowing all the answers, able to convey genuine curiosity and openness to thoughtful contributions from a wide variety of sources, and able to facilitate students' own critical analyses and creative constructions.*

Across the three projects, instructors promote active learning by structuring high levels of student involvement. Students are asked to contribute their experience and ideas, critique the provided curriculum materials, gather and discuss information from local sources and gather new data. Ultimately, they are asked to construct concepts and practice models informed by this generated curriculum. Instructors increase the personal relevance and social applicability of what is taught by recruiting large numbers of knowledgeable and respected members of students' local communities to generate curriculum content and learning activities, and to play an active role in teaching. Students ask community members both pre-planned and spontaneous questions about their academic subject matter. At the same time, instructors structure individual and small group learning activities and assignments that engage students with 'mainstream' textbooks and course manuals representing established Western knowledge on the subject. Instructors facilitate the evolution of a 'community of learners' in which students, community members, and the instructor engage in critical discussion, debate, expansion, and application of the indigenous and the university-based curriculum content.

## Example 1: Students Constructing Malay Mental Health

An opportunity to explore participatory pedagogy and to incorporate indigenous knowledge occurred during my decade of teaching in Malaysia when there were a number of partnerships between American universities and regional post-secondary institutions serving rural communities. Inspiration for the pilot project came from students enrolled in an American undergraduate program delivered in Malaysia. All of the students were Malay, Iban or Dayak. Most were devout Muslims from small rural communities. My role was to teach a psychology course that all students were required to take, using a curriculum prescribed by the American university. Students 'complained' that many of the questions that have preoccupied Western social scientists throughout the history of psychology were not important and sometimes had no meaning within their rural, Muslim, collectivist context. In essence, they asked how they could be expected to engage in learning about research and theory on child-rearing, family life, personality types, social behavior, and mental health among mostly white, middle-class people in North America. In particular, they noted that concepts, interventions and outcome measures described in their textbooks on the topic of 'mental health' had little or no applicability to the social structure, expectations and practices in their own communities. This was especially of concern, since an education and social development priority in Malaysia at that time was to train young people for clinical, counseling and community mental health practice. The students sought and welcomed opportunities to undertake information-gathering assignments that would bring cultural and context-relevant information into an otherwise largely irrelevant curriculum. We decided to focus on the area of mental health with a fresh approach to teaching and learning.

*Communities of learners can also create new knowledge that is culturally and contextually appropriate. Students can experience a high degree of agency in determining what they learn and how they learn it. Their education can reflect the settings in which they live and intend to work.*

The innovation, which came to be a regular part of the psychology course, was aimed at a student-driven elaboration of culturally consistent, community-appropriate concepts and practices for promoting 'well-being'. First, students and cultural 'informants' in the students' communities compiled, catalogued and critiqued local (*emic*) beliefs, concepts and prevalent practices to promote, protect and restore 'mental wellness'. Second, this 'community of learners' engaged in an exploration and critique of North American (*etic*) concepts, programs of research and 'best practices' pertaining to 'mental health and illness'. Finally, the learners developed a framework (*derived etics*) for their own inquiries and for applying a hybridized indigenous-Western approach to developing capacity for community service in the area of mental wellness (Ball, Muzlia, & Moselle, 1994).

This initiative yielded insights that guided my involvement in the two more recent pilot projects:

1. Ensuring the relevance and usefulness of curriculum across varying cultural and community contexts means more than being 'culturally sensitive' and acknowledging the possibility that what we teach may have limited generalizability. Rather, it means leaving

a significant space for the 'unknown' in course curriculum, where students can identify what they want and need to learn.

2.  Similarly, being accountable to local supporters of education in order to meet local goals for social development means opening up the foundations of curriculum to include locally generated questions and the means for answering them using local resources. Together with local advisors, avenues for helping students to meet their own learning goals and broader social development goals can be found to bring to the fore context-relevant curriculum content.

3.  Students will mobilize their curiosity, creativity, critical thinking and capacity for generating new knowledge when they are given significant roles in creating and constructing at least part of the curriculum.

4.  Students, instructors and participating community members can experience transformative learning through teaching and learning processes that lead to the evolution of a 'community of learners' rather than the reinforcement of overly rigid and anachronistic expert-learner-layperson distinctions.

## Example 2: Demonstrations of a Generative Curriculum Model

The second pilot project that effectively combines participatory learning and incorporation of indigenous knowledge was initiated by indigenous communities in Canada. In Canada, the term 'indigenous people' currently refers to the original inhabitants of the land, and includes First Nations (formerly called Indian or native people), Inuit, Aleut and Metis population groups. In North America, mainstream training programs have yielded low rates of retention and completion among indigenous students (Assembly of First Nations, 1988; Battiste & Barman, 1995). As a result, indigenous people are under-represented in all professional and academic fields. There is increasing recognition that for many indigenous students, there is neither intrinsic nor extrinsic motivation to learn the overwhelmingly white, middle-class content or to engage in the types of learning activities found in mainstream post-secondary programs (Wilson, 1994). Many educators have argued that curricula need to incorporate indigenous philosophies, languages, and practices (Assembly of

First Nations, 1988; Battiste & Barman, 1995), and that pedagogical models need to be developed that ensure equity between 'insider' and 'outsider' knowledge frames (Lockhart, 1982).

The pilot project, which is ongoing, consists of the evolution and demonstration of a 'Generative Curriculum Model' for co-constructing and co-delivering a post-secondary program in child and youth development and care (Pence & McCallum, 1994). The project, housed at the University of Victoria, enables the delivery of post-secondary training in indigenous communities, through partnerships between indigenous community groups and the university (Pence & Ball, 1999). Over the past decade, there have been eight partnership programs using the Generative Curriculum Model. The programs have been delivered in very small, remote communities with just 10 students, and in larger urban centres with 23 students in a learning cohort. More information about this initiative is available at www.fnpp.org.

This pilot project started with the assumption that culturally valued and useful knowledge about childhood and child care is embedded within the community and that this knowledge needs to be afforded a central place in the development of training curricula. At the same time, indigenous community partners have asserted that there is value in considering the perspectives and knowledge yielded by Euro-Western research, theory and professional experience. This biculturally respectful stance has laid the foundation for 'communities of learners' to become engaged in co-constructing culturally grounded training curricula that combine the best of both worlds. A recently completed evaluation of this project yielded clear evidence of unprecedented successes for students, the partnering communities and the post-secondary institutions involved (Ball, 2001). The project is unique in Canada with regard to the extent of community involvement and incorporation of cultural knowledge.

## Inside the Generative Classroom

The Generative Curriculum Model places special demands on instructors. Generative curriculum development begins with ensuring that the privilege of knowledge is diffused. Inviting community members as collaborators in co-constructing curricula and placing culturally embedded constructs at the core—rather than at the periphery—of education has profound implications for educators. This approach affects the kinds of questions we ask about the roles of teachers and students as agents of learning, cultural articulation and social development.

How do instructors facilitate the development of a curriculum that is co-constructed with community members? In the evaluation of this project, 19 instructors, each of whom taught in one of the partnership programs, offered accounts of their experiences using the Generative Curriculum Model. Their accounts underscore how their teaching differs from how they were trained to teach and from prevailing teacher-driven approaches to post-secondary pedagogy. They emphasize that their ability to diverge is essential to realizing the generative and transformative potential of the Generative Curriculum Model. As a way to capture these differences, the instructors were asked to formulate 'advice' for future instructors aiming to teach generatively. The following is what they listed.

1. Respect the cultural and historical experience of community members as valuable sources of knowledge, rather than affording authority only to Western theories, research, and practices.

2. Become familiar with the priorities, practices and circumstances of the community, without becoming involved in them. In the pilot projects, the university-based partners and the instructors did not seek or presume to become experts or insiders of the cultures or social life of the community partners.

3. Respond flexibly to expressions of students' and community needs regarding the program.

4. Ground teaching and learning in consideration of many viewpoints, rather than relying principally on the modernist approach of 'universal' truths and 'best practices' in human services. Instructors need to be self-critical and willing to jettison the 'excess baggage' of their own mainstream training and their own cultural 'blinders'.

5. Be receptive to what the community brings to the project, although these contributions may come in unfamiliar forms and at unexpected times.

6. Accept 'not knowing' where an informed discussion might lead, rather than maintaining the colonialist presumption of 'knowing' what is true and best for all people and relying on pre-packaged curricula developed by 'experts'.

7. Avoid 'doing' when non-action would be more productive of student agency and community participation. Assume an encouraging, non-directive stance while waiting.

8. Be prepared to join in the 'community of learners' as an authentic participant, and be receptive to being transformed as thoroughly as are the students.

Using the Generative Curriculum Model, what is taught and what is learned takes a different shape each time a curriculum is taught, reflecting the unique knowledge that resides in the local community and the experiences of the students.

> It [the Generative Curriculum Model] highlights the importance of the learning process, collaboration, and participation. The result is a holistic experience, grounded in the social context.
>
> Instructor, Nzen'man' Partnership Program

For most instructors in the pilot project, it is the first time they experience working with an indeterminate curriculum and it is challenging.

> When the classes started, I felt like an experienced "rookie". I had never taught generatively before and I felt like I was sitting backwards at my desk.
>
> Instructor, Meadow Lake Tribal Council Program

Each course has a scripted "course pack" created by a university-based team, representing about 50% of the course content. Since context-specific indigenous knowledge is usually not available in written form, instructors rely on participation in curriculum development and teaching by respected cultural informants recruited from the community. Their contributions are often the catalysts for the creative development of new ways of uncovering, organizing, generating and testing knowledge that is relevant to the program context. In most indigenous communities in Canada, Elders are the traditional teachers of younger generations and they are the main repositories of cultural knowledge. Thus, in the partnership programs, Elders contribute significant portions of the content of each course. In some partnerships, curriculum is also generated by younger, respected community members who have first-hand experience with the culture, language, and social practices of students' communities.

> Elders were invited to co-instruct and help with the Generative Curriculum process. They brought with them their wisdom from the accumulation of their lifetime experience and knowledge. We learned together. Each Elder had his or her own special knowledge. We had an Elder who coordinated

the Elders' participation. He knew which Elder to ask for which days of the course, based on who had the most cultural knowledge and experience about the topic we were covering.

Instructor, Meadow Lake Tribal Council Program

Instructors report staying alert in every course for opportunities to: (a) involve Elders and other knowledgeable community members in teaching activities (b) integrate teachings gleaned from community members into the course work and (c) encourage students to reflect on the words of community contributors throughout their class discussions, assignments, and practicum activities. In addition to course content, the Elders usually model ways of storytelling and listening, encouraging sharing and facilitating the elaboration of ideas and action plans that are themselves expressions of indigenous cultures.

It started out that the Elders sat at the front of the class and all the students were at their tables and the Elders kind of chatted to us from up there. The students took notes and it was very much like a classroom situation. Then the Elders said: 'This isn't the way we do this. We don't talk this way, as us and them. And it's disrespectful while we're speaking for peoples' heads to be down like this and writing. We talk in a circle. There's all these tables between us and there's no interaction, there's no real connection happening there.' It was a turning point for our class. We made changes that created more of a sharing kind of situation and it really began to feel like a learning community.

Instructor, Meadow Lake Tribal Council Program

Instructors often encounter differences in how understandings are created and the process by which understandings are tested and generalized.

Knowledge, as I have experienced it, is often derived from outside myself; that is, information is objectified, logical, and provable. Listening to the Elders and other community members, knowledge for them appears to be generated from within oneself, and set within the context of their reality.

Instructor, Meadow Lake Tribal Council Program

For most instructors, it is the first time they put the knowledge and experience of students, Elders, and other community members at the forefront in class discussions.

With the indigenous way of learning, you always try to go from local to national to international. It was important for the students first to know about the topics from an indigenous viewpoint, and then learn about national policies and programs, and then learn about international programs of research, theories, and practice models.

Instructor, Nzen'man' Program

Instructors make an effort to 'lead with the local' knowledge first. Knowledge provided in glossy textbooks often has an intimidating effect on students and community members, who may feel that their words can never be as worthy as the words on the printed page imported from abroad.

I've always thought of adult learners as being contributors, but never quite so much as being contributors first - asking what they know first and then going to the textbook or other type of material second.

Instructor, Meadow Lake Tribal Council Program

Instructors, who are usually not members of students' cultural communities, do not attempt to become 'experts' in indigenous ways of knowing.

An instructor from outside the culture that the students are from can never really know what the students' experiences have been like, or the experience of living in their communities. You can visit, you can work there every day, and still not have awareness of many things. It is really important to be aware of not knowing and to be open to learning from the students.

Instructor, Tl'azt'en Nation Program

Instructors play a key role in facilitating the discussion of various perspectives and sources of knowledge.

What I wanted for human services as an instructor was probably less important than what the Elders and other members of the students' own communities were saying to them and what their own ideas were. We integrated all those ideas. We didn't all envision the same things, but they were all valuable things for them to consider in becoming effective human service workers.

Instructor, Meadow Lake Tribal Council Program

Instructors do not sift, censor, evaluate, or attempt to modify knowledge contributed by students and community contributors. In order to teach 'generatively,' instructors need to be open to realities that differ from their own and they need to value the knowledge and experience of students.

> I spent the first 3 months learning how to listen, how to provide a climate of trust—a safe place where esteemed community members could feel respected and appreciated for the knowledge they imparted, and a safe place where students could learn new information and assess the value of that information in the context of their own life experiences. As an instructor, I too felt empowered by this process.
>
> Instructor, Cowichan Tribes Program

Instructors typically report that they become more open, reflective, and responsive in their teaching styles.

> The key thing that improved me as an instructor was I learned to wait. I learned not to expect immediate answers, immediate feedback, and to give things a chance, wait for the relevance to emerge. Sometimes people would say something that didn't seem relevant to the discussion and then I would figure out later on that it was really relevant and that the students could quite often see this relevance before I could. I learned to look for messages in different ways too. Sometimes students would use humour to give me a message that something was not relevant for them or that what I thought an Elder had intended to communicate was not what they understood from the same communication.
>
> Instructor, Cowichan Tribes Program

The Generative Curriculum Model requires the instructor to help students make connections in the 'space between' the emergent, indigenous curriculum and the university-based, scripted curriculum.

> Quite often the students would feel like what the Elder said had contradicted something I had been teaching. So, then it was up to me to put it all together on my feet. You really had to be listening in the Elders' teaching session and be thinking as you went, anticipating what this is going to turn into by the next morning. I needed to be ready for my class because those would be the moments when you could really help students to make the connections and comparisons between the indigenous knowledge and the research-based knowledge.
>
> Instructor, Meadow Lake Tribal Council Program

The Generative Curriculum Model involves a 'lived' learning. Providing information and knowledge alone would not produce the breadth of learning that the generative, community-inclusive approach provides.

> What began to happen was an awareness that instruction isn't just here in the classroom. This learning is having an impact on lives, and lives were outside of the classroom. Learning is not neutral and information is not neutral. It has impact, it has meaning, it has motion. The instructional process is far more than a kind of radio beacon: it's not simply the transmitter and the receiver operating independently.
>
> Alan Pence, University of Victoria,
> Pilot Project Co-Coordinator

After considering the scripted course content and the contributions of community members and students, each student is free to select, blend, integrate, or reconstruct perspectives in order to create their own unique perspective. However, they are expected to be able to provide a compelling rationale for their choices, informed by content that has come into the generated curriculum through the inputs from the university, community, or student body.

> One of the things that really struck me is the ability of the students to think analytically and critically. Not only did their academic skills, in terms of their reading and writing and confidence increase, but they also became willing to pick things apart, examine the elements, and reconstruct things in often creative and useful ways. You could see the wheels turning all the time. And what we hear now from the students who are at a 4th-year level, working on their degrees, is that they are influencing the mainstream classroom, and modeling how to critique concepts, bring in culturally based knowledge, and start creating new forms of knowledge. I think that we just challenged them so much to think about theory in terms of its relevance to their own communities and so they became very skilled.
>
> Instructor, Cowichan Tribes Program

Overall, many of the behaviors and attitudes that instructors emphasize are also emphasized in research on effective education. Several investigators have attributed student satisfaction and success to teaching strategies that allow students to have a voice in making curriculum decisions and in sharing their experience and knowledge (Battiste & Barman, 1995; Steffe & Gale, 1995). Investigators have reported greater gains in learning and performance when instructors are facilitators of learning rather than disseminators of knowledge (Robertson 1996). There is increasing interest among investigators in strategies of educational program delivery, such as the 'community of learners' approach pioneered by Rogoff (1990), that are inclusive of the broader community.

The pilot project with indigenous communities in Canada has involved cohorts not exceeding 23 students. However, if instructors are skilled in the use of cooperative learning, such as described by Jacobs and Loh in chapter 10 of this book, it is feasible to use the Generative Curriculum Model in education programs with larger groups. The effectiveness of this approach would seem to depend less upon the size of the class, and more upon the instructor. The instructor needs to be comfortable with not knowing all the answers, able to convey genuine curiosity and openness to thoughtful contributions from a wide variety of sources, and able to facilitate students' own critical analyses and creative constructions.

## Example 3: Early Childhood Development Virtual University in Africa

The third pilot project explores 'generative curriculum' with a slightly larger student cohort. It also explores the use of learning technology as part of an array of teaching and learning strategies. Initiated by my colleague, Alan Pence, this project is a post-graduate program to support the development of African leaders in early childhood development and care. More information about this project is available at http://www.ecdvu.org.

A cohort of 33 specialists in social education and health policy and programs in 11 African nations are enrolled in the first pilot of this project, which has just begun. Courses combine virtual learning, face-to-face seminars, and community consultation in Africa. A primary goal of African and international sponsors of this initiative is that leaders will emerge with capacities to direct policy and program development that is responsive to local contexts and informed both by indigenous knowledge bases and by findings from Western research and practice.

Following principles of 'generative' teaching and learning, instructors (including myself) engage students in individual and group-based learning activities that involve: (a) structured and systematic student-led uncovering of sources of information and ways of knowing about the determinants of child development in their own eco-cultural work contexts (b) consideration of Western theories, research methods, findings and practice models pertaining to child development and (c) creation of new knowledge about child survival and development in specific geocultural regions in Africa. A program of research will assess the degree to which this innovative approach achieves its 'generative' goals.

## Concluding Comments

The pilot projects described in this chapter suggest the value of an indeterminate, generated approach to curriculum that invites multiple perspectives on a subject matter and especially emphasizes indigenous knowledge and experiences. Participatory teaching practices that encompass the broader social community can create new communities of learners who are encouraged to study and evaluate various sources of knowledge with respect to their potential applicability in local contexts. Communities of learners can also create new knowledge that is culturally and contextually appropriate. Students can experience a high degree of agency in determining what they learn and how they learn it. Their education can reflect the settings in which they live and intend to work. The first two pilot projects have demonstrated successes in terms of student performance and contributions to social development goals. The projects suggest some guidelines for educators interested in securing the relevance and meaningful productivity of programs in tertiary level institutions and development assistance programs within a larger postmodernist, anti-colonialist agenda. Dennis Esperanz, an indigenous educator who played a key role in implementing one of the partnership programs in Canada, commented:

> We educators have to be visionaries, but when we talk curriculum, we also have to consider the vision of people in our communities—what their goals are. The Generative Curriculum Model contains a larger vision of how to bring the two different visions together—the one that academics see and the one that guides people out there in the communities. So we've learned a new approach to making what we do here [in this institution] meaningful and effective for all parties. People are just starting to understand what this is all about.

# References

Assembly of First Nations. (1988). Charleston, G.M. (Ed.) (1988). *Tradition and education: Towards a vision of our future* (2 vols). National Review of First Nations Education. Ottawa, Canada: Assembly of First Nations.

Ball, J. (1994). Strategies for promoting active learning in large classes. *Journal of Teaching Practice, 2,* 3-11.

Ball, J., Muzlia, S., & Moselle, K. (1994). Cultural influences on help-seeking for emotional problems in Malay communities. In G. Davidson (Ed.), *Applying psychology: Lessons from Asia and Oceania* (pp. 97-112). Carlton: Australian Psychological Society Press.

Ball, J. (1998). Identity formation in Confucian-heritage societies. In P. Pedersen (Ed.), *Multiculturalism as a fourth force.* (pp. 147- 165). Philadelphia: Taylor and Francis, Bruner/Mazel.

Ball, J. (2001). *First Nations Partnership Programs—Generative Curriculum Model. Program evaluation report.* Victoria, Canada: University of Victoria.

Battiste, M., & Barman, J. (1995). *First Nations Education in Canada: The circle unfolds.* Vancouver, Canada: UBC Press.

Becker, J., & Varelas, M. (1995). Assisting construction: The role of the teacher in assisting the learner's construction of preexisting cultural knowledge. In L. Steffe and J. Gale (Eds.), *Constructivism in education* (pp. 433 – 446). Hillsdale, N.J.: Lawrence Erlbaum.

Dahlberg, G., Moss, P., & Pence, A. (1999). *Beyond quality in early childhood education and care: Postmodern perspectives.* London: Falmer Press.

Freire, P. (1993). *Pedagogy of the oppressed* (M. Bergman Ramos, Trans.). New York: Continuum.

Giroux, H. (1992). *Border crossings: Cultural workers and the politics of education.* New York: Routledge.

Ki-Zerbo, J., Kane, C.H., Archibald, J., Lizop, E., & Rahnema, M. (1997). Education as an instrument of cultural defoliation: A multi-voice report. In M. Rahnema & V. Bawtree (Eds.), *The post-development reader* (pp. 152-160). London: Zed Books.

Lather, P. (1991). *Getting smart: Feminist research and pedagogy within the postmodern.* London: Routledge.

Lockhart, A. (1982). The insider-outsider dialectic in native socio-economic development: A case study in process understanding. *Canadian Journal of Native Studies, 2,* 159-162.

Pence, A., & Ball, J. (1999). Two sides of an eagle's feathers: Co-constructing ECCD training curricula in university partnerships with Canadian First Nations communities. In H. Penn (Ed.), *Theory, policy and practice in early childhood education* (pp. 36-47). Buckingham, UK: Open University Press.

Pence, A., & McCallum, M. (1994). Developing cross-cultural partnerships: Implications for child care quality, research, and practice. In P. Moss & A.

Pence (Eds.), *Valuing quality in early childhood services: New approaches to defining quality* (pp. 108-122). New York: Teachers College Press.

Robertson, D. L. (1996). Facilitating transformative learning: Attending to the dynamics of the educational helping relationship. *Adult Education Quarterly, 47*(1), 41-53.

Rogoff, B. (1990). *Apprenticeship in thinking: Cognitive development in social context.* New York.: Oxford University Press.

Shiva, V. (1997). Western science and its destruction of local knowledge. In M. Rahnema & V. Bawtree (Eds.), *The post-development reader* (pp. 161-167). London: Zed Books.

Smith, L.T. (1999). *Decolonizing methodologies: Research and indigenous peoples.* London: Zed Books.

Steffe, L.P., & Gale, J. (1995). *Constructivism in education.* Hillsdale, NJ: Lawrence Erlbaum Associates.

Wilson, P. (1994). The professor/student relationship: Key factors in minority student performance and achievement. *Canadian Journal of Native Studies, 14* (2), 305-317.

http://www.ecdvu.org (accessed Nov. 2001)

http://www.fnpp.org (accessed Nov. 2001)

# About the Author

**Jessica Ball**, Ph D, is a professor of cross-cultural developmental psychology in the School of Child and Youth Care at the University of Victoria, Canada. She spent a decade in Southeast Asia, where she was involved in teacher training, schooling to support development of the 'whole child', school-based research on youth risk behaviors, and cross-cultural mental health. Confronted with abundant evidence of the erosion of indigenous cultures as a result of importation of Western pedagogical, youth development, and counseling approaches, Jessica has spent the past decade exploring ways to bring indigenous knowledge into focus in education and human services, while also supporting community-development agendas for selective adaptation of imported ideas. Working with colleagues in Canada, Jessica has pioneered a 'Generative Curriculum Model'. She has evaluated the effectiveness of this approach in Aboriginal communities. She is currently involved in an adaptation of the model in a distributed learning Masters degree program in Early Childhood Care and Development in sub-Saharan Africa. Jessica Ball has also conducted extensive comparative research on identity formation and risk behaviors among adolescents. E-mail: jball@uvic.ca.

# CHAPTER 7

# Including Students with Disabilities within Mainstream Education

*Levan Lim, Cherry Ko, Serene Choi & Rebecca Ireland*

The winds of change are clearly evident in many countries around the world in the new millennium. The notion of a *shared future* is very real in this new world order. There is nothing as critical as the education of the young that affects the course of this shared future. Many governments appear to have recognised this and pursue strategic alignment between how the young are educated and the desired future of societies. In this global climate, the idea of a separate education is becoming increasingly contentious. Governments, including those in developing countries, and major world organisations (like UNESCO) are aiming to reach and include as many children as possible, especially the disadvantaged, those in poverty and those with disabilities, within mainstream education.

In this chapter, we address the significance of including children with disabilities within mainstream education. In the first half of this chapter, we provide an overview of what inclusive education is about, its international profile and existing practices in various parts of the world. We refer to developing countries where the reality of large classes of students has not deterred the successful inclusion of students with disabilities. Instead, inclusive practices in developing countries disconfirm the conventional Western-based suggestion that inclusion is mainly possible in small classes. In the second half of the chapter, we introduce practical approaches and strategies that mainstream teachers can adopt and adapt to facilitate the inclusion of children with disabilities within their classrooms.

## Inclusive Education: Philosophy and Rationale

Inclusive education, or inclusion, believes that everyone should learn, grow, live and work with others of similar and diverse backgrounds in regular, mainstream environments, whether these are schools, work settings or community sites. Inclusion, according to Strully and Strully (1996), brings together all children and adults in order to learn to recognise and appreciate the unique gifts each individual brings. In educational circles, inclusion or inclusive education is associated with the idea of educating students with disabilities in mainstream schools alongside with regular peers. Although commonly used to refer to school contexts, inclusion is fundamentally concerned with establishing caring and welcoming communities for all within society. Inclusion is different from integration in that the latter seeks to prepare students with disabilities to fit into or adapt to mainstream schools without the necessary assumption that schools need to change to accommodate a greater diversity of students (Mittler, 2000).

The inclusion of students with disabilities within mainstream classes has been shown to produce better educational and social outcomes for all children (Baker, Wang, & Walberg, 1994/1995; Banerji & Dailey, 1995; Hunt & Goetz, 1997; Manset & Semmel, 1997; Staub & Peck, 1994/1995). The common argument that having students with disabilities in regular classes will have adverse effects on students without disabilities has been refuted by research (Holloway, Salisbury, Rainforth & Palombaro, 1994; Sharpe, York & Knight, 1994). On the contrary, research has highlighted the benefits of inclusion for students without disabilities in terms of reduced fear of human differences, increased comfort and awareness, enhanced cognition and self-concept, greater sensitivity to individual differences, development of personal principles, and warm and caring friendships (Staub & Peck, 1994/1995).

*Inclusion is not about reproducing best special school practices and approaches within mainstream schools.*

The key to successful inclusion is the responsible and thoughtful interpretation and implementation of inclusive practices. Inclusive practices, adapted from The PEAK Parent Center's list (Power-deFur & Orelove, 1997) of inclusive practices are as follows:

1. The school has a philosophy that respects all students as learners and contributing members of the classroom and school community and holds the highest aspirations for all students.
2. Students attend the mainstream school and class they would attend if they did not have disabilities, following the same schedule as other students and receiving support services in or out of the classroom.
3. Mainstream education classes have a natural proportion of students with and without disabilities in the class (approximately 10 to 15% of students in the class).
4. Students with disabilities receive the support they need to be successful in the classroom (e.g., curriculum adaptation and modification, assistive technology, adult and peer assistance).
5. Teachers who have students with disabilities in their classrooms receive the support necessary for them to teach all students in their class successfully (e.g., planning time, consultation and collaboration with specialists and parents, classroom support, training).
6. Parents of students with disabilities are given every opportunity to be full participants in their child's education.
7. As a new educational practice, planning and training precede implementation.

## The International Profile of Inclusion

Inclusion has become a progressively prominent international agenda for improving the lives of children around the world. A number of international initiatives concerning all children, such as The Salamanca Statement (UNESCO, 1994), The Standard Rules on the Equalisation of Opportunities for Disabled Persons (United Nations, 1993), and The United Nations (1989) Conventions on the Rights of the Child emphasize the improvement of educational opportunities for the world's children with reference to the inclusion of children with disabilities within these initiatives.

The Salamanca Conference organised in 1994 by the United Nations Educational, Scientific and Cultural Organisation (UNESCO) and the government of Spain produced the most explicit international statement so far concerning the inclusion of children with disabilities. Representatives of 92 governments and 25 international organisations agreed upon a statement—the UNESCO Salamanca Statement

(1994)—calling for inclusion to be the norm for the education of all children with disabilities. This conference was unprecedented in its clarity and scale: it not only spelled out the philosophy and practice of inclusion but also resulted in a commitment to inclusive education by governments around the world. The Salamanca Statement states that "experience in many countries demonstrates that the integration of children and youth with special educational needs is best achieved within inclusive schools that serve all children within a community. It is within this context that those with special educational needs can achieve the fullest educational progress and social integration" (UNESCO, 1994, p. 11).

## Inclusion Experiences in Developing Countries

> In fact one of the lessons of the past decade is that so-called developing countries have much to teach richer countries about inclusion.
>
> Mittler, 2000, p. 28

Besides reasons grounded in humanitarian, moral and social justice foundations, the case for inclusive education for many countries around the world is based on reasons of cost, sustainability, maximum outreach, community impact and proven effectiveness.

Many developing countries are not able to afford the costly development of a separate infrastructure of specialists and special education services for a relatively small number of children with disabilities. Even if funds were obtained to initially finance the building of a separate infrastructure, the amount of resources required to sustain the level of effectiveness of such a system for as many children as possible over a long term would not be possible. Developing countries simply cannot afford to (and should not) follow the earlier direction of many wealthier developed countries that have created a separate educational infrastructure to cater to the needs of children with disabilities that they are now in the process of attempting to dismantle in order to provide more inclusive opportunities for all children.

The issue of reaching out to as many children with disabilities as possible in developing countries can be hampered by a separate system where limited resources are skewed towards funding a separate education with limited places which may only be accessed by those who can afford a place in such a system. For example, in Morocco, Stubbs (1997) described the contrast between those children with disabilities who have a separate special education and those who do not receive any education. Stubbs mentioned a special school of children with physical disabilities that catered to around 120 students with cost per child per year of $1,200 when there were about 1 million children with disabilities in Morocco who did not receive any education. In addition, when the children from the special school moved on to attend secondary school, they often experienced ridicule, pity, overprotection and isolation from peers not used to the experience of disability. In another case, in Papua New Guinea, in 1992, before the advent of inclusive education, only 94 children with disabilities were registered as receiving schooling in the whole country (Enabling Education Network, 1999). Building a separate system to educate the needs of students with disabilities is simply not a feasible option in many developing countries.

Responsible inclusive principles and practices demand that relevant community contexts and resources be carefully understood and engaged with in order to effectively involve the community in supporting inclusion. This community-based feature of inclusion, known by its widespread use of the term "community-based rehabilitation" (CBR), facilitates the indigenisation of inclusive education to be situated within local communities. There are many communities in developing countries that have sustained traditional care-taking beliefs and practices for people with disabilities, such as extended family and community supports and networks, which can be built upon.

It has been shown that greater familial, school and community involvement towards "owning" the inclusion of all children leads to successful efforts regardless of whether a country has a developing or developed status. In fact, the experiences in developing countries

*The revelation that inclusion can be successful in class sizes of between 50 to 100 children is mind-boggling yet indicative of the "resiliency" of the concept of inclusion in its interpretation and "doability" in various cultural contexts. While most Western-based texts strongly suggest that inclusion occurs best in small classes, this example of inclusive practices defy conventional wisdom and knowledge about inclusion.*

appear to contain insights into inclusive education for the developed countries to learn about. According to Stubbs (1996), despite few material resources, limited access to information and large class sizes, many developing countries have examples of excellent policy and practice in inclusive education because: i) they are not hindered by a legacy of segregation; ii) there is more community solidarity; and iii) they have more expertise in utilising existing local resources.

Let's consider the issue of class size, which seems to be a key point of teachers with respect to implementing inclusive practices in their classrooms. It is common to find that Western-based literature on inclusive education (e.g., Blenk & Fine, 1995) recommend class sizes be kept small (below 25 students) for successful inclusion to occur. Small class sizes are however not a viable option in countries where large class sizes (40 and above) are the norm because of a shortage of teachers, inadequate resources, or because large numbers of students have always been the traditional class size. If it were the case that small classes are prerequisite to successful inclusion, inclusion would only be limited to a minority of countries in the world.

## Inclusive Education in Lesotho

The case of inclusive education in Lesotho, a country surrounded by the Republic of South Africa, provides an excellent testament to the fact that inclusion can occur in large classes. Amidst major economic and social problems faced by this African nation, education has been pursued as a priority for all children. A pilot project that included local children with disabilities within mainstream classes was launched in 1993 in response to the country's commitment to the United Nations Education for All Initiative. Teachers in the selected schools were given training over an intensive three-week period (Khatleli, Mariga, Phachaka and Stubbs, 1995). In a follow-up evaluation report of the project by Mittler and Platt (1995), these researchers found that the teachers were for the most part highly successful in including children with disabilities in the regular mainstream classroom, in spite of class sizes of 50 to 100 students! What was observed in their evaluation was a range of teaching strategies that included multi-level or differentiated curriculum, small group work, peer mediated interventions as well as one-to-one work. Students with disabilities were not separated from their peers without disabilities and both were observed to be on task as well as being socially and educationally involved.

The Lesotho experience highlights inclusive education not just as a viable educational route to reach as many children as possible but also as a sustainable school practice that naturally builds upon the inclusiveness of its culture. The revelation that inclusion can be successful in class sizes of between 50 to 100 children is mind-boggling yet indicative of the "resiliency" of the concept of inclusion in its interpretation and "doability" in various cultural contexts. While most Western-based texts strongly suggest that inclusion occurs best in small classes, this example of inclusive practices defy conventional wisdom and knowledge about inclusion. In addition, the Lesotho experience strongly suggests the significance of the cultural context in redefining and reinterpreting different forms and practices of inclusion. What predisposed the teachers of such large classes in Lesotho to be described as "naturally inclusive" (p. 27) is an interesting question that leads to Mittler's perspective that so-called developing countries have much to teach the richer and developed countries about inclusive education:

> There are classrooms with up to 100 children in many parts of the world that are inclusive because each lesson and each activity seems naturally created to ensure that all the children can take part. By the same token, one can find classes with two adults and 20 children in which a few children are literally and metaphorically at the margins, not taking part in the lesson and isolated from other children.
>
> Mittler, 2000, p. 177

Mittler and Platt's evaluation of Lesotho's pilot project to include children with disabilities within mainstream schools stated that the inclusive practices they observed were attributed more to the teachers' natural teaching skills rather than the training received. This observation supports the notion that teachers' attitudes towards including children with disabilities are fundamental to successful inclusion. Teachers' attitudes are, in turn, grounded and framed by their own cultures and experiences. The teachers in the Lesotho project were genuinely motivated by a sense of community responsibility, religious conviction and humanitarianism (Stubbs, 1996).

Stubbs (1996) described how inclusion was extended to a child with cerebral palsy in the Lesotho project. The child had been identified through the programmes and had started to attend school once a wheelchair had been obtained from the local clinic. She made progress not just academically but in terms of her basic self-help skills and overall confidence. Then the wheelchair broke and no one knew how to repair it. The community had gained from seeing her improvement and was concerned for her. A neighbour lent a wheelbarrow and other school children pushed her to school. Then the neighbour needed the wheelbarrow back and she was stuck at home once again. But the connection had been made: the teachers visited her and sent older children to teach her and her friends to visit her at home.

Mittler's (2000) reflections on his observations of inclusive education in Lesotho as well as other countries such as Hong Kong and Bangladesh, where large class sizes are the norm, led him to conclude that the skills and abilities of teachers in mainstream classes are the natural foundations upon which inclusion can be built.

## Inclusive Practices for Mainstream Classrooms

Inclusion is primarily an issue associated with mainstream educational school reforms (Gable & Hendrickson, 1997; Mittler, 1995). Inclusion is not about reproducing best special school practices and approaches within mainstream schools. On the contrary, inclusion is about improving the education of students with disabilities within broader educational reform efforts to improve education for all students (Kochhar & West, 1996). Inclusion implies a radical reform of schools in terms of curriculum, assessment, pedagogy and student grouping (Mittler, 2000). For inclusive education to be implemented on a system-wide level, there are various levels to address, such as the ministry or district level, the school or building level as well as the classroom level. Investments at each level are important to sustaining a comprehensive system of support efforts to facilitate proactive planning and tackling of emerging issues as well as meaningful change (Fullan, 1993). Although many factors and levels are involved in the implementation of a comprehensive and effective system of inclusion, mainstream teachers are left with the primary

*Inclusion is different from integration in that the latter seeks to prepare students with disabilities to fit into or adapt to mainstream schools without the necessary assumption that schools need to change to accommodate a greater diversity of students (Mittler, 2000).*

task and responsibility of teaching students. Therefore, even without the enforcement or endorsement of inclusive education at the system's level, the inclusion of students with disabilities at the classroom level can still take place if teachers embrace learning and teaching approaches and practices that have been shown to reach all students.

Besides the willingness and attitudes of mainstream teachers towards including students with disabilities, the effectiveness of inclusion at the classroom level also largely depends on the use of learning and instructional approaches and practices that can include all students. In developing countries like Lesotho where large class sizes reign, and in the cases of many Western countries where much smaller class sizes are the norm, there are a number of inclusive approaches and practices that can be implemented in classrooms regardless of whether class sizes are large or small.

## A Coherent and Interdisciplinary Curriculum

In a coherent and interdisciplinary curriculum, there is a strong recognition that problems and issues that arise in daily or real-life situations require a combination or integration of skills that cuts across disciplines to solve. For example, preparing for a job interview requires one to dress appropriately (aesthetics), polish up one's resume (editorial skills), find the site of the interview (map reading and literacy skills), tell the time and figure out the approximate time needed to get to the interview in time (maths), answer questions (listening and verbal skills), be friendly and able to carry a conversation (social skills), etc. Learning is referenced to the demands of the real environments students are likely to find themselves in. In a coherent/interdisciplinary curriculum, students are "consciously guided to see, discuss, internalise, and then discover the nature of the connections in what they are studying" (Palmer, 1995, p. 56). Such a curriculum benefits those students with disabilities who have problems retaining information and knowledge, generalisation and transfer of skills and seeing the interrelationships between what they are studying.

## Multilevel Instruction

According to Collicot (1991), in multi-level instruction, the teacher should:

- Consider student learning styles when planning formats for displaying learning.

- Involve students in the lesson at appropriate levels of thinking and cognition. For example, a student with a severe disability could learn to identify the names of materials (knowledge) in a science class while his or her classmates attempt to understand and apply the use of the materials.
- Adjust expectations of some students' performance and level of participation. For example, the objective for a student may be partial participation where the student does part and not all of an activity. A child with limited mobility may not be able to chase a basketball but be allowed to practice throwing into the net.
- Let students choose which methods they use to convey understanding of concepts taught. A child with limited nonverbal communication and who likes computers could choose to type answers to demonstrate learning. Accept that these different methods are valid.
- Evaluate students based on individual differences and abilities. For example, a student who can be evaluated for reading comprehension by acting out or putting up a performance to illustrate a story instead of an oral narration.

Adapting levels of instruction for various abilities and skills within a single lesson can also occur across curricular areas. This happens when lesson planning is such that curricular areas overlap to address the needs of some students within a single class session. For example, a student with a severe disability can identify names of materials in a science period and also count the number of peers present (maths) and identify the names of peers for roll call for the teacher by matching faces to pictures with names attached (literacy and social cognition skills). Creativity is needed to find ways to include students with disabilities through a variety of instructional and learning opportunities within the classroom environment.

## Cooperative Learning

Cooperative learning approaches have been found to work well with efforts to include students with disabilities within classroom groups (Putnam, 1998). In cooperative learning situations, students learn skills such as positive interdependence, individual accountability, dealing with differences and interpersonal and friendship skills (Nevin, 1998; Putnam, 1998; Slavin, 1995). George Jacobs and Loh Wan Inn describe cooperative learning strategies in further detail in chapter 10 of this book.

# Peer-mediated Instruction

Peer-mediated instruction refers to the use of peers to tutor and instruct each other in classroom learning activities. This is a powerful way of reaching all students in large classes, as shown in the Lesotho pilot project example. There are a number of peer-mediated strategies which have been used successfully for effective classroom teaching and learning for all students, including students with disabilities.

*Peer Modeling*   A peer is available to model appropriate behaviours to a less skilled child. Peer modelling has worked with children with withdrawn behaviours, autism, behaviour problems and intellectual disability (Mathur & Rutherford, 1991; McHale, 1983).

*Peer Initiation Training*   Peers are trained to evoke and maintain desirable social and communicative behaviours from a student. Behaviours taught with children with disabilities include establishing eye contact, offering or asking for help and display of affection (Odom, Strain, Karger & Smith, 1986; Storey, Smith & Strain, 1993).

*Peer Monitoring*   Peers assist by being buddies to their peers to help them perform tasks with less assistance from the teacher. Preschoolers have acted as buddies for their peers with autism to make transitions around the classroom (Carden-Smith & Fowler, 1984; Fowler, 1986; Sainato, Strain, LeFebvre & Rapp, 1987).

*Peer Networking*   Groups of students form a positive system of support to encourage appropriate social and behavioural responses from particular peers. Teachers can train peers to prompt and encourage particular peers (e.g., peers with autism) to learn and engage in social interaction skills (Kamps, Leonard, Vernon, Dugan & Delquadri, 1992; Ostrosky & Kaiser, 1995).

*Peer Tutoring*   Peers act as instructors to provide individualized instruction, practice, repetition, and clarification of concepts. Peer tutors clarify prescribed tasks, give feedback and provide reinforcement for correct performance (Foot, Shute, Morgan & Barron, 1990; DuPaul & Henningson, 1993).

## Conclusion

The inclusion of students with disabilities in mainstream classes is a significant agenda for many countries around the world. Western countries like the United States, Canada and Britain have produced a large body of literature advocating the philosophy of inclusion and documenting its successful practices. Inclusive practices in these countries, however, take place in relatively small class sizes. In addition, the literature and practices from these countries strongly recommend and emphasize small class sizes. Many so-called developing countries have also turned to inclusion as a viable route to improving educational opportunities for as many children as possible. Class sizes in these countries are much larger than those in Western countries and emerging evidence from around the world show that inclusion in such settings is possible. Successful inclusive experiences in both types of countries have one thing in common—the use of particular approaches and practices that seek to include all students, including those with disabilities, within mainstream classes. We encourage teachers reading this chapter to take time to reflect on their own personal values and willingness in relation to inclusion. Teachers have a powerful role in determining the future of inclusion in schools and, in turn, the future of inclusion of all citizens in society.

## References

Baker, E., Wang, M., & Walberg, H. (1994/1995). Synthesis of research: The effects of inclusion on learning. *Educational Leadership, 52,* 33-35.

Banerji, M., & Dailey, R. (1995). A study of the effects of an inclusion model on students with students with learning disabilities. *Journal of Learning Disabilities, 28,* 511-522.

Blenk, K., & Fine, D. L. (1995). *Making school inclusion work: A guide to everyday practices.* Cambridge, MA: Brookline.

Carden-Smith, L. K., & Fowler, S. A. (1984). Positive peer pressure: The effects of peer monitoring on children's disruptive behavior. *Journal of Applied Behavior Analysis, 17,* 213-227.

Collicot, J. (1991). Implementing multi-level instruction: Strategies for classroom teachers. In G. L. Porter & D. Richler (Eds.), *Changing Canadian schools: Perspectives on disability and inclusion* (pp. 191-218). Toronto, Canada: G. Allan Roeher Institute.

DuPaul, G. J., & Henningson, P. N. (1993). Peer tutoring effects on the classroom performance of children with attention deficit hyperactivity disorder. *School Psychology Review, 22,* 134-143.

Enabling Education Network, United Kingdom (1999). *Case study: Papua New Guinea. The provision for children with hearing impairment and deafness in an 'inclusive' system.* Retreived from http://www.eenet.org.uk.

Foot, H. C., Shute, R. H., Morgan, M., & Barron, A. M. (1990). Theoretical issues in peer tutoring. In H. C. Morgan, M.J. Shute, & R. H. Shute (Eds.), *Children helping children* (pp. 59-92). New York: John Wiley & Sons.

Fowler, S. A. (1986). Peer-monitoring and self-monitoring: Alternatives to traditional teacher management. *Exceptional Children, 52,* 573-583.

Fullan, M. (1993). *Change forces: Probing the depths of educational reform.* London: Falmer.

Gable, R. A., & Hendrickson, J. M. (1997). Teaching all students: A mandate for educators. In J. S. Choate (Ed.), *Successful inclusive teaching: Proven ways to detect and correct special needs* (2nd ed.) (pp. 2-17). Needham Heights, MA: Allyn & Bacon.

Holloway, T. M., Salisbury, C. L., Rainforth, B., & Palombaro, M. M. (1994). Use of instructional time in classrooms serving students with and without severe disabilities. *Exceptional Children, 61,* 242-253.

Hunt, P., & Goetz, L. (1997). Research on inclusive educational programs, practices, and outcomes for students with severe disabilities. *Journal of Special Education, 31,* 3-29.

Kamps, D. M., Leonard, B. R., Vernon, S., Dugan, E. P., & Delquadri, J. (1992). Teaching social skills to students with autism to increase peer interactions in an integrated first-grade classroom. *Journal of Applied Behavior Analysis, 25,* 281-288.

Khatleli, P., Mariga, L., Phachaka, L., & Stubbs, S. (1995). Schools for all: National planning in Lesotho. In B. O'Toole, & R. McConkey (Eds.), *Innovations in developing countries for people with disabilities* (pp. 135-160). Chorley, UK: Lisieux Hall Press.

Kochhar, C. A., & West, L. L. (1996). *Handbook for successful inclusion.* Gaithersburg, MD: Aspen.

McHale, S. (1983). Social interventions of autistic and nonhandicapped children during freeplay. *American Journal of Orthopsychiatry, 53,* 81-91.

Manset, G., & Semmel, M. (1997). Are inclusive programs for students with mild disabilities effective? A comparative review of model programs. *Journal of Special Education, 31,* 155-180.

Mathur, S. R., & Rutherford, R. B. (1991). Peer-mediated interventions promoting social skills of children and youth with behavioural disorders. *Education and Treatment of Children, 14,* 227-242.

Mittler, P. (1995). Special needs education: An international perspective. *British Journal of Special Educationa, 22,* 105 – 108.

Mittler, P. (2000). *Working towards inclusive education: Social contexts.* London: David Fulton Publishers Ltd.

Mittler, P., & Platt, P. (1995). *Evaluation of Integration Pilot Programme in Lesotho.* Report to Save the Children Fund (UK) and Ministry of Education, Lesotho.

Nevin, A. (1998). Curricular and instructional adaptations for including students with disabilities in cooperative groups. In J. W. Putnam (Ed.), *Cooperative learning and strategies for inclusion, 2nd ed.* (pp. 49-65). Baltimore: Paul H. Brookes.

Odom, S. L., Strain, P. S., Karger, M. A., & Smith, J. D. (1986). Using single and multiple peers to promote social interaction of preschool children with handicaps. *Journal of the Division for Early Childhood, 10,* 53-64.

Ostroksy, M. M., & Kaiser, A. P. (1995). The effects of a peer-mediated intervention on the social communicative interactions between children with and without special needs. *Journal of Behavioral Education, 5,* 151-171.

Palmer, J. M. (1995). Interdisciplinary curriculum—again. In J. Putnam (Ed.), *Cooperative learning and strategies for inclusion: Celebrating diversity in the classroom* (pp. 41-56). Baltimore: Paul H. Brookes.

Power-de Fur, L.A., & Orelove, F.P., (1997). Inclusive education: Practical implementation of the least restrictive environment. Gaithersburg, MD: Aspen Publishers.

Putnam, J. W. (1998). *Cooperative learning and strategies for inclusion, 2nd ed.* Baltimore: Paul H. Brookes.

Sainato, D. M., Strain, P. S., LeFebvre, D., & Rapp, N. (1987). Facilitating transition times with handicapped preschool children: A comparison between peer-mediated and antecedent prompt procedures. *Journal of Applied Behavior Analysis, 20,* 285-291.

Sharpe, M., York, J., & Knight, J. (1994). Effects of inclusion on the academic performance of classmates without disabilities. *Remedial and Special Education, 15,* 281-287.

Slavin, R. E. (1995). *Cooperative learning (2nd ed.).* Needham Heights, MA: Allyn and Bacon.

Staub, D., & Peck, C. (1994/1995). What are the outcomes for non-disabled students? *Educational Leadership, 52,* 36-40.

Strully, J., & Strully, C. (1996). Friendships as an educational goal: What we have learned and where we are headed. In S. Stainback & W. Stainback (Eds.), *Inclusion: A guide for educators.* (pp. 141-154) Baltimore: Paul H. Brookes.

Stubbs, S. (1996). Poverty and membership of the mainstream: Lessons from the south (Can poverty facilitate inclusion?). Retreived from http://www.eenet.org.uk.

Stubbs, S. (1997, July). *Towards inclusive education: The global experience of Save the Children (UK).* Paper presentation at the 2nd Ibero-American Special Education Congress (Special Education Requirements and their Challenges for the 21st Century), Havana, Cuba. Retreived from http://www.eenet. org.uk.

Storey, K., Smith, D. J., & Strain, P. S. (1993). Use of classroom assistants and peer-mediated interventions to increase integration in preschool settings. *Exceptionality, 4,* 1-16.

United Nations (1989). *Convention on the rights of the child.* New York: United Nations.

United Nations (1993). *Standard rules on the equalisation of opportunities for disabled persons.* New York: United Nations.

UNESCO (1994). *The Salamanca statement and framework for action on special needs education. World conference on special needs education: Access and quality.* New York: UNESCO.

# About the Authors

**Levan Lim**, Ph D, is a lecturer at the Schonell Special Education Research Centre, the University of Queensland, Brisbane, Australia. Levan grew up in Malaysia and has lived and worked in Singapore, Canada, the United States of America and Australia. With a doctorate in special education, his current research interests include cross-cultural collaboration between parents and professionals within special education, autism, person-centred planning, community development and inclusion. Levan was recently involved in an AusAid-funded project to promote the inclusion of children with disabilities in the Philippines. Email: l.lim@mailbox.uq.edu.au.

**Cherry Ko** is a Masters candidate at the Schonell Special Education Research Centre of the University of Queensland, Australia. Her research topic focuses on how a primary school in Brisbane promotes and practices inclusion.

**Serene Choi** is a doctoral candidate at the Schonell Special Education Research Centre of the University of Queensland, Australia. Her dissertation examines the use of peer-mediated interventions to promote social interactions between students with autism and their regular peers in school settings.

**Rebecca Ireland** is a doctoral candidate at the Schonell Special Education Research Centre of the University of Queensland, Australia. Her dissertation topic focuses on choice and quality of life for individuals with developmental disabilities.

# CHAPTER 8

# Reaching Children of High Ability

*Thana Thaver*

My greatest learning lesson in teaching highly able children still remains my first encounter with them. Armed to the teeth with all of 3 years of teaching experience, I entered the class supremely confident. Only pride carried me out of the room at the end of the lesson, spine ramrod straight.

Are highly able children different? Do they have different needs? How can a teacher meet their needs in a large class setting with pupils of mixed ability? In this chapter, I attempt to give you a thumbnail portrait of these children—like all snapshots, they only capture a certain facet of these children, and even then, there will be variation in different children. Along with the characteristics, I will also try to delineate some of the concomitant problems that may arise because of their giftedness. In closing, I will share some practices that enhance the learning of these children.

## A Thumbnail Portrait of Highly Able Children

What first struck me about these children is their motivation and task commitment (Davis & Rimm, 1998; Rogers, 1986). Given any challenging task, these children become the teacher's dream class. They get right into the task with minimum fuss once they have understood it and will persist at it until they have completed it. The ability to concentrate for long periods of time aid them. This, however, can pose problems for teachers in the classroom. The almost compelling desire to complete tasks may be so strong in some of these children that they continue with their work right into the next teacher's lesson, thereby causing disciplinary problems.

In addition to task persistence, there may be exhibited in a number of these children the tendency towards perfectionism (Davis

& Rimm, 1998; Alderholdt-Elliot, 1989). Their high expectations and fear of failure may cause them to take twice as long in any assigned task, creating feelings of stress, and in some cases, the inability to meet deadlines. In extreme forms, this can translate into an inability to start on the task. This behaviour is often seen in the gifted under-achiever, and is usually misconstrued as laziness rather than a crippling fear.

*Why do I dwell on the story of Robin? In a large class setting, it is so easy for the Robins of this world to slip through the cracks and never fulfil their potential. It is a loss for him and a loss for society.*

I remember one such child. There was no doubt that Robin (not his real name) was a bright child. He possessed leadership qualities, was vocal in class and occasionally showed sparks of intellectual potential beyond his age group. However, Robin never delivered. He rarely handed in his work without the teacher reminding him, and when he did, it was usually shoddy and obviously done in a hurry. Despite the close supervision of his teachers, Robin continued on his merry way, seemingly uncaring of the poor grades he was obtaining, and unaware of the anger he was generating with his attitude. After working with Robin and his parents, we realized that one of the problems plaguing Robin was his excessively high expectations and his feelings of being overwhelmed. This caused him to delay starting any task and when he finally did, it had to be done in a rush. To preserve his self-esteem, he would justify his bad grades by saying that if he had put in more effort, he would have done better. Ironically this would have been true: he had the capacity. However, Robin, so caught up in his coils of fear, could not see this and did not know how to ask for help. By the time, we caught on to this pattern of behaviour and understood his motivations, it was deeply entrenched.

Why do I dwell on the story of Robin? In a large class setting, it is so easy for the Robins of this world to slip through the cracks and never fulfil their potential. It is a loss for him and a loss for society. We often do not take notice of the quiet Robins who do just enough to get by because of the sheer numbers of pupils we are dealing with, and their more obvious learning and disciplinary problems.

It, thus, becomes incumbent on us to know the children we teach and to use this knowledge to shape our interactions with them, to look beyond the surface to the source. With experience and a constantly probing mind, we will develop a certain sensitivity and a talent for spotting pupils with special needs, especially important in a large class setting.

Another noticeable trait of highly able children is their deep hunger for content that is complex and stimulating, which they acquire and process with amazing speed (Tannenbaum, 1983; Feldhusen, 1989). Their intellectual precocity, their ability to think independently and abstractly (Van Tassel-Baska, 1994; Delisle, 1997) and their desire to engage in intellectual debate creates an environment that can be tremendously exciting or conversely, intimidating for the teacher unused to or not very confident with such learners.

*In that instant, I realized that my traditional notions of teacher as a dispenser of knowledge had to change. I needed to learn to be a facilitator to give them room to grow intellectually, within agreed upon behavioural boundaries.*

A lesson I well remember that first gave an insight into the minds of these children was one I had prepared on a fairly complex poem in my first month of teaching them. I discovered before long that I had underestimated their intellectual capacity and their ability to take over my lesson. They plunged enthusiastically into the discussion of themes and motifs, arguing belligerently with their peers and me, the teacher, offering insights and interpretations I had never even thought of. In that instant, I realized that my traditional notions of teacher as a dispenser of knowledge had to change. I needed to learn to be a facilitator (Hutlgren & Seeley, 1982; Nelson & Prindle, 1992), to give them room to grow intellectually, within agreed upon behavioural boundaries.

I also found, to my amusement, that if their needs were not met, the bolder pupils had no compunctions about expressing their unhappiness, verbally or non-verbally. A teacher working with these children truly needs strong ego strength to meet the intellectual challenge posed by these children in the classroom (Feldhusen, 1985).

## Provisions for Highly Able Learners

In many countries, it is still the belief that highly able children can be fully served in regular classroom settings. Unfortunately, the curriculum in the regular classroom is generally not tailored to meet the needs of these pupils, and teachers make no effort to modify instructional strategies or materials to challenge the highly able (Archambault, Westberg, Brown, Hallmark, Zhang & Emmons, 1993). The responsibility of nurturing these learners lie with classroom teachers whose pre-service training would not normally have prepared them for recognizing the gifted, especially the underachieving gifted, or in the instructional methods suited for meeting the needs of these children. These teachers also receive very little or no support in terms of in-service training and curriculum materials (Larsson, 1990; Boxtel, 1992; Lovecky, 1994).

Little attention is paid to gifted children because it is often strongly felt that they need no special provisions because their high ability enables them to 'look after themselves' and pre-programmes them to success (Colangelo & Davis, 1997). There seems little realization or belief that giftedness is developmental in nature, and that any number of factors in the environment like an inadequate curriculum or unsuitable instructional methods, social and emotional difficulties, pressures within the home and school can affect and even extinguish the development of these children's abilities (Davis & Rimm, 1998; Gallagher, 1991; Cornell, Callahan & Lloyd, 1991).

In Singapore, provisions for highly able children came at a time when the government perceived the need to educate its best and brightest to meet its future needs, politically and more importantly, economically. The educational model adopted was one of special enrichment classes within regular schools, which were already serving this population. Pupils would be selected for these classes through specially administered tests. In these classes, the curriculum would be differentiated to meet their intellectual needs, and the teachers further trained to understand the nature and needs of these children and to modify their instructional methods.

Research seems to show that highly able learners benefit academically from this kind of ability grouping (Kulik & Kulik, 1997). However, to see significant gains in student achievement, there must be accompanying curricular adjustments. Kulik & Kulik (1997) also report that benefits are usually largest in special self-contained accelerated and enriched classes.

It would be ideal indeed for all learners, especially those with special needs, to be placed in small classes of between 15 and 20 pupils. In such settings, research seems to indicate that there is a related increase in student achievement and positive reports on the parts of students, teachers and parents on the improved quality of classroom activity (Pritchard, 1999). Smaller class sizes allow for more individualized attention to students, greater flexibility in terms of different instructional approaches and assignments (Mosteller,

*This brings us to the crux of the matter. Whether the needs of highly able children are met, ultimately, is not dependent on class size but really on the effectiveness of their teachers and the teachers' willingness to make provisions for them in the classroom.*

1995; Kickbusch, 1996) and a more relaxed, interactive learning environment with better classroom management.

However, reducing class sizes does not necessarily guarantee more effective teaching and greater increase in student achievement. Indeed, Greenwald, Hedges and Laine's work (1996) seems to indicate that teacher expertise is one of the more important factors in determining student achievement. The research study demonstrated the relative impact of spending $500 more per pupil on increased teacher education, increased teacher experience and increased teacher salaries, and found that all three appeared to have greater impact on student test scores than does lowering pupil-teacher ratio.

In addition, research also indicates that most teachers do not change their practices or make only slight changes to the ways they covered the curriculum and the types of activities employed when they moved to smaller classes (Bohrnstedt & Stecher, 1999). Thus, even if class size is reduced, professional development is still essential not only to help teachers adopt more effective instructional strategies but also to maximize the opportunities provided by smaller class sizes.

This brings us to the crux of the matter. Whether the needs of highly able children are met, ultimately, is not dependent on class size but really on the effectiveness of their teachers and the teachers' willingness to make provisions for them in the classroom.

How then does a teacher meet the needs of highly able learners whether in a small or large class setting? Here, I share some elements which, in essence, transcend any type of class setting or learner but which are crucial if a teacher is to reach highly able children. They are the ability of the teacher to *differentiate instruction* to meet the needs of the gifted and create a learning *environment* in which they can thrive in, and his/her *attitude* towards teaching and learning.

## Differentiating Instruction to Meet the Needs of Highly Able Learners

In a large-class setting, curriculum can be differentiated to cater to the different readiness levels, ability, interests and learning style preferences of students. The teacher would use a variety of ways to enable students to explore curriculum content, a variety of activities through which learners can process and understand the content presented, and a variety of options in which students can demonstrate what they have learnt (Maker, 1982; Maker & Nielson, 1996). For highly able learners, these components of the curriculum should be enriched and/or accelerated depending on their needs.

According to Van Tassel-Baska (1997), the following characteristics should shape teaching and learning in a classroom with highly able learners:

a) The curriculum should emphasise depth over breadth and concepts over facts. All students should be exposed to the key concepts of the subject being studied. While struggling learners are helped to grasp and use the concepts, highly able learners should be encouraged to further expand their understanding and application of the ideas. Understanding and transformation are stressed rather than retention and regurgitation. The role of the teacher in this classroom would be to provide various learning options to facilitate learning at different paces and depth.

b) The curriculum would also incorporate higher order thinking in all subject areas and provide opportunities for pupils to reflect on, monitor and assess their own learning processes. It also seeks to develop habits of minds through cultivating thinking that resemble those of professionals in the various fields, in terms of skills, attitudes and dispositions.

c) There would be on-going and authentic assessment to further individualise and tailor instruction as well as to involve learners more actively in the learning process.

d) Flexible grouping arid differentiated assignments would be consistently used. In the differentiated classroom, students will work in different grouping arrangements, sometimes alone, sometimes in pairs or groups. Whole class instruction is used to introduce new content or for sharing products of students. In addition, tasks set are also differentiated, in terms of abilities, interests or learning style preferences.

e) Pupils in these classrooms are seen as active explorers. The teacher's role is to be a facilitator of learning rather than a dispenser of content knowledge. The curriculum would promote active learning and problem solving. The teacher must be competent in his/her subject as well as in the management of learning. The teacher has to, thus, give much thought to designing the conditions/structures needed to facilitate student-centred learning in a large class setting and teaching students responsibility for their own work.

## Creating a Supportive Learning Environment

The fate of the gifted lies in the hands of the teacher, for "it is the teacher who sets the environment which inspires or destroys self-confidence, encourages or suppresses interest, develops or neglects abilities, fosters or banishes creativity, stimulates or discourages critical thinking, and facilitates or frustrates achievement" (Nelson & Cleland, 1971, p.439).

Besides being strong in their content area and possessing knowledge of instructional strategies suited to developing the gifted, teachers of highly able children must have knowledge of the nature and needs of the children they teach. This will enable them to understand the challenges and problems associated with giftedness (some of which were shared at the beginning of the chapter).

Highly able learners need teachers who are emotionally stable with strong ego strength, who are flexible and able to adapt and find ways to deal with the stress and exceptional behaviour of these children (Mulhern & Ward, 1983). They need teachers who are able to provide a warm, safe and permissive environment in which they can be stimulated intellectually and encouraged to take risks in learning (Tannenbaum, 1983). As with all learners, there is a need to emphasise the role of effort in learning by focusing on process and progress, and to sacrifice accuracy, occasionally, for risk-taking. This is vital in the light of the gifted learner's tendency towards perfectionism and their internal pressure to always be successful.

Finally, for highly able learners to perform at optimal levels, they require teachers with high achievement motivation who will not only have high expectations of their learners but also of themselves. The lessons they garner from such role-modelling are priceless. This was brought home with clarity to me when a young gifted child once shared with me why he felt the need to work hard. It was to live up to his mother. He greatly loved and admired his mother because she worked very hard, juggling the demands of her 'office work', studying for a degree and making a home for him and his brother.

## Attitude of the Teacher towards Teaching and Learning

To be an excellent teacher, there must be passion—a passion for knowing, both what is in the field and outside, passion for the craft of teaching and a passionate concern for the children you work with (Hulgren & Seeley, 1982).

*Passion for knowing is a habit of the mind; it is a curiosity about and a wonder at the world and how it works. As you exude this, you will find that not only are you engaging the learners in what you teach but modelling for them another important disposition.*

This trait is one that you will share in common with gifted children. You will find that highly able children are often children with passion. They have interests in areas that are unusual or more like the interests of older children, and they can be non-conforming and driven in the pursuit of their learning and interests (Davis & Rimm, 1998; Rogers, 1986).

Passion for knowing is a habit of the mind; it is a curiosity about and a wonder at the world and how it works. As you exude this, you will find that not only are you engaging the learners in what you teach but modelling for them another important disposition. For gifted children, you will strike a chord of 'likeness' as well, making them feel that they may have found a kindred soul (Lovecky, 1994).

## Conclusion

In conclusion, I would like to reiterate that an open and flexible teacher, willing to make modifications to meet the needs of his/her learners would be an effective teacher whatever the class setting and type of learner. What will truly make a difference to the pupils you teach will be the fact that you regard each and every one of them as gifted in his or her own right and deserving of the best you can give.

## References

Adderholdt-Elliot, M. (1989). Perfectionism and underachievement. *Gifted Child Today, 12(1)*, 19-21.

Archambault, F. X., Westberg, K. L., Brown, S., Hallmark, B. W., Zhang, W., & Emmons, C. (1993). Regular classroom practices with gifted students: Findings from the classroom practices survey. *Journal for the Education of the Gifted, 16*, 103-119.

Borhrnstedt, G. W., & Stecher, B. M. (1999). (Eds.). *Class size reduction in California: Early evaluation findings, 1996-98.* Palo Alto, CA: CSR Research Consortium.

Boxtel, H. W. Van (1992). Final report. In F.J. Monks, M. W. Katzko, & H. W. van Boxtel (Eds.), *Education of the gifted in Europe: Theoretical and research issues* (pp. 22-43). Amsterdam: Swets and Zeitlinger.

Colangelo, N., & Davis, G. A. (1997). (Eds.), *Handbook of gifted education* (2nd ed). Boston: Allyn & Bacon.

Cornell, D. G., Callahan, C. M., & Lloyd, B. H. (1991). Socioemotional adjustment of adolescent girls enrolled in a residential acceleration program. *Gifted Child Quarterly, 35*, 58-66.

Davis, G. A., & Rimm, S. B. (1998). *Education of the gifted and talented.* Needham Heights, MA: Allyn & Bacon.

Delisle, J. R. (1997). Gifted adolescents: Five steps towards understanding and acceptance. In N. Colangelo and G. A. Davis (Eds.), *Handbook of gifted education* (pp. 475-482). Boston: Allyn & Bacon.

Feldhusen, J. F. (1985). The teacher of gifted students. *Gifted Education International, 3(2)*, 87-93.

Feldhusen, J. F. (1989). Why the public schools will continue to neglect the gifted. *Gifted Child Today, 12(2),* 55-59.

Gallagher, J. J. (1991). Personal patterns of underachievement. *Journal for the Education of the Gifted, 14,* 221-233.

Gallagher, J. J. (1997). Issues in the education of gifted students. In N. Colangelo & G. A. Davis (Eds.), *Handbook of gifted education* (pp.14-23). Boston: Allyn & Bacon.

Greenwald, R., Hedges, L. V., & Laine, R. D. (1996). The effects of school resources on student achievement. *Review of Educational Research. 66(3),* 361-396.

Hultgren, H. W., & Seeley, K. R. (1982). *Training teachers of the gifted: A research monograph on teacher competencies.* Denver CO: University of Denver, School of Education.

Kickbusch, K. (1996). *Class size.* Madison, WI: Wisconsin Education Association Council, Professional Development Division. Retrieved from www.weac. or/resource/may96/classize/htm.

Kulik, J. A., & Kulik, C.-L. C. (1997). Ability Grouping. In N. Colangelo & G. A. Davis (Eds.), *Handbook of gifted education* (pp. 230-242). Boston, MA: Allyn & Bacon.

Larsson, Y. (1990). Teachers' attitudes and perspectives on educational provisions for "Gifted" and "Talented" children in New South Wales, Australia and Essex, England. *Gifted Education International, 17(2),* 131-142.

Lovecky, D. (1994). Exceptionally gifted children: Different minds. *Roeper Review, 17(2),* 116-120.

Maker, C. J. (1982). *Curriculum development for the gifted.* Austin, TX: Pro-ed.

Maker, C. J., & Nielson, A. B. (1996). *Curriculum development in the education of the gifted.* Austin, TX: Pro-ed.

Mosteller, F. (1995). The Tennessee study of class size in the early school grades. *The Future of Children, 5(2),* 113-127.

Mulhern, J.D., & Ward, M. (1983). A collaborative program for developing teachers of gifted and talented students. *Gifted Education Quarterly, 27* (4), 152-156.

Nelson, J., & Cleland, D. (1971). The role of the teacher of gifted and creative children. In P. Witty (Ed.), *Reading for the gifted and creative student.* Newark, DE: International Reading Association.

Nelson, K. C., & Prindle, N. (1992). Gifted teacher competencies: Ratings by rural principals and teachers compared. *Journal for the Education of the Gifted, 15,* 357-369.

Pritchard, I. (1999). *Reducing class size: What do we know?* National Institute on Student Achievement, Curriculum and Assessment. Office of Educational Research and Improvement. U.S. Department of Education. Retrieved from www.ed.gov/pubs/ReducingClass/Class_size.html.

*Policy Report on Class Size.* ERIC Clearing house on Educational Management. College of Education, University of Oregon. Retrieved from http://eric. uoregon.edu/publications/policy_ reports/class_size on 2 Nov 2001.

Rogers, K. B. (1986). Do the gifted think and learn differently? A review of recent research and its implications. *Journal for the Education of the gifted, 10(1),* 17-40.

Tannenbaum, A. J. (1983). *Gifted Children.* New York: Macmillan.

Van Tassel-Baska, J. (1994). *Comprehensive curriculum for gifted learners* (2nd ed.). Boston: Allyn & Bacon.

Van Tassel-Baska, J. (1997). What matters in curriculum for gifted learners: Reflections on theory, research, and practice. In N. Colangelo & G. A. Davis (Eds.), *Handbook of gifted education* (pp.126-135). Boston, MA: Allyn & Bacon.

## About the Author

**Thana Thaver** is a teacher educator at the National Institute of Education of the Nanyang Technological University, Singapore. She is an experienced secondary school teacher and has taught in the Gifted Education Programme in Singapore. For nearly a decade, Thana Thaver was with Singapore's Ministry of Education as a Gifted Education Specialist. She was involved in developing the primary school English curriculum for the gifted, supervising and training teachers of the gifted and in testing and assessment. Thana Thaver grew up in Malaysia before she moved to Singapore as a young adult. E-mail: tlthaver@nie.edu.sg

# CHAPTER 9

# Teacher-student Relationships in Large Classes

*Doris M. Martin*

Any group of people anticipating spending nearly a year together and meeting on an almost daily basis is naturally curious about each other. Who is this teacher? Who are these students? The relationships that develop between teachers and students significantly affect the teaching and learning processes. Yet, the topic rarely receives attention in either the "how to" or the theoretical discussions of teaching. Despite the lack of research and formal attention to the quality and nature of these relationships, teachers and students are concerned with how they relate to each other. Teacher-student relationships are central to the quality of experiences of both teacher and students. Creating relationships with students, in the context of supporting students' construction of knowledge, increases the likelihood of social and academic success for students as well as the personal and professional satisfaction of teachers (Pianta, 1999). The challenge for the teachers of large classes is in getting to know and in relating to many students at the same time.

When I consider my first teachers, I recall some with great affection and appreciation and others who I wished had not been part of my life. The following examples represent both perspectives. One morning, my friend and I missed the school bus and had to walk to school. We arrived very late and cautiously entered the classroom in the middle of a lesson. Sheepishly, we took our seats. Sensitive to our embarrassment at arriving late, Mrs Huber did not call attention to us and never even mentioned the incident. Her trust in us and our respect for her had evolved throughout the year in countless ways. For instance, after lunch and the noon recess every day, Mrs Huber read a new chapter to us while we rested our heads on our desks. There were no accompanying quizzes, assignments or other extrinsically motivating activities. There were no threats that we should "pay attention" or else. The pure enjoyment and suspense of well-crafted children's literature read by a woman we respected and who respected us supported our intrinsic motivation to listen and to learn.

By contrast, when I was 15, I attended a new high school and was assigned to a math teacher who, I believed, did not care whether I learned algebra. To me, he was sarcastic and demeaning. He frequently used class time for discussions unrelated to the subject. I considered his class a waste of my time. As if to punish him, I stopped doing my homework and seldom studied. Instead, I focused on subjects where teachers were cordial and made me and other students feel like we were their "reason for being". One could easily argue that at age 15, I should have been able to separate my feelings for the teacher from the benefits of doing well in school. While this is true, my point is that teachers have a responsibility to convey to students that the students are important regardless of lessons learned or unlearned.

In this chapter, I will discuss teachers' relationships with their students from the perspective of the caring constructivist teacher. Teacher-student relationships form even without the teacher's awareness and conscious effort. However, working to create meaningful and satisfying relationships between teachers and students requires *getting to know each other, building trust, nurturing and caring*, and *expecting the best*. These four aspects correspond roughly to the four needs—*intrusion, structure, nurturance* and *challenge*—that Austin De Laurier claimed must be met if children are to develop into healthy and socially competent individuals (Jernberg, 1981). Examining relationships across these four areas can help teachers to consciously create balanced and healthy relationships. Such relationships support students' social cognition, knowledge that is needed for the rest of students' lives.

## The Nature of Teacher-student Relationships

Teachers' relationships with students follow different patterns and take on different levels of meaning and importance according to the teacher's own school experiences, the teachers' training and philosophy of education and the particular milieu of the classroom. Each person—each teacher and each student—brings his or her own history of relationships into each social interaction. In chapter 4 of this book, Richard Blunt recognizes Waldorf teaching as an art that involves the teacher coming to terms with him or herself. Teachers as well as students have temperaments that must be factored into relationships. The expressions of our temperaments are shaped by the interactions we have had with early caregivers. Early on, we construct patterns of interactions that simultaneously effect our ideas of who we are in relationship to others (Main, Kaplan & Cassidy, 1985). For example, a child whose caregiver(s), usually a parent, is not responsive or available to the child, is likely to believe that he or she is not worthy of adults' attention or care (Bretherton & Waters, 1985). This sense of "unworthiness" serves as a mental model for subsequent interactions with other adults as well, e.g. the teacher (Bretherton, Ridgeway & Cassidy, 1987). A student, expecting a teacher to be like earlier adults he or she has known, will act according to the earlier model. Determined that the world is as they expect it to be, such students will work until they are successful in getting the teacher to react in the same negative or punitive way that he or she is accustomed to.

Zeke, who was doing poorly in school, was a bully to fellow students and was disrespectful to the teacher. Despite Mr Teacher's efforts to be cordial, Zeke continued to make comments just out of the teacher's hearing to provoke the laughter of his classmates. In frustration, Mr Teacher screamed at Zeke and told him to leave the room. Zeke had succeeded in angering the teacher and had finally succeeded in getting the kind of response that he expected from adults, confirming once more his negative expectations for himself and others. Mr Teacher did not want to react in anger, but Zeke had learned from many previous encounters that sooner or later most adults would loose control if Zeke pushed long enough. The relationship developed between Zeke and his teacher was not the kind that will support Zeke in changing his attitude toward school, nor would this relationship likely be satisfying for Mr Teacher.

The pattern of relationships that Zeke forced upon his teachers reinforced an interaction pattern that had probably been in place much of Zeke's life. The creative, caring teacher must find a way to break the cycle and get to know Zeke well enough to engage him in solving their mutual problem. The process of restoring Zeke's trust in others is likely to be long and arduous and will likely require encounters outside the traditional classroom context.

Teachers and students are affected by and affect the other person as they co-create an evolving dyadic relationship. While both participate in creating the relationship, the teacher by virtue of his or her role, age and experience, generally has more power and certainly more responsibility to set the direction and quality of the relationship (Hartup, 1989). This is not to deny the very powerful behaviors that children learn very early on in effecting the interactions between them and the adults in their lives. The case of Zeke illustrates the power that students/children can and often do exert in their relationships with teachers or even parents. The challenge for teachers is to firmly but gently claim their roles as the ones responsible or the "ones in charge" and, thus, reassure those students who have grown up with adults whom they could not count on (Jernberg, 1981).

## Viewing the Class as a Whole

Each group of students, no matter what the context, assumes a sort of personality of its own based on the specific blend of people in the group. Despite differences within the group, the group identity can become a strong and persistent lens by which the teacher comes to view the group. I have frequently heard teachers describe a class as "immature" or "advanced" or "difficult". In using these terms, we tend to forget that the class is made up of individuals. Classifying the group according to a dominant portion of the group can lead to stereotyping of the class and to conducting ourselves as teachers as if everyone were the same. We can avoid this by focusing our attention on getting to know the individual members of the group.

## Getting to Know Every Child

Getting to know someone begins with acknowledgment of the others' existence. All of us want to be seen, to be known, to be recognized as persons worthy of others' attention. Pediatrician and researcher, T. Berry Brazelton (Brazelton & Greenspan , 2001) tells us the importance of nurturing that takes place as the infant gazes into the parents' eyes. We feel validated in being seen by a friendly and significant other. This being "seen" is not merely looking; rather this kind of "seeing" by the other is full of positive regard for the individual. Seeing in this regard is in no way threatening and makes no demands. It conveys that as I see you, I value you just as you are and I find satisfaction in the gift of your presence.

I experienced two very different approaches from children while as a stranger I observed in their preschool classroom. A 3-year-old boy ran up to me and rather brusquely demanded that I hold some of his "weapons" as he darted around the room using them in wildly imaginary and evocative play. He returned momentarily to exchange items, but never engaged me further or included me in his play except as a repository for his weapons. Later, I noticed another child peer cautiously up at me from the paper that she was coloring. We made eye contact and I smiled briefly. A few minutes later, she approached me saying, "This is for you," as she handed me a self-portrait. I thanked her and in the brief exchange felt validated by this small stranger. By contrast, the other child seemed not to have been aware of me as a person. I was conveniently available to hold his stock. He looked at me only to see whether I was willing to comply with his demand and after that resumed his play seemingly oblivious of me. These simple exchanges, both initiated by young children, illustrate two very different styles in relating with adults. While it is unfair to assume that these encounters are representative of each of these children, as weapon holder, I felt objectified. In contrast, as recipient of a self-portrait, I felt that I had been entrusted with a very personal gift, an opening for building trust and furthering an I-Thou relationship.

Getting to know another involves a bit of intrusion, that is we "intrude" on another by either asking them to reveal themselves, or we share information about ourselves and "intrude" on the other with expectations that they will receive what we give to them. One young teacher confided that when she was at a party or meeting strangers, she never initiated contact with others for fear that they did not want to be bothered by her. She was unsure of her worthiness and did not want to risk being rejected (Martin, 1991). However, in her role as teacher, she recognized how essential it was for her to initiate connection with her young students. Students who are shy or lacking in confidence need teachers who provide gentle ways of letting the students know that they are worth knowing (Collins, 1996). Our first interaction with every student must convey that we value him or her as a person.

Students who are unable to respond to or to initiate positive social interactions with peers or adults, need a wise teacher who will take

*When a teacher vows to greet every student with a kind word, positive acknowledgment, a smile, the teacher does not do so with the idea that these behaviors will change the student, but with the assurance of changing oneself. When the teacher is changed, the students will change.*

the initiative in getting to know them and patiently support them in developing alternative ways of being among others. For example, the child who becomes recognized as the class "clown" making other students laugh at inappropriate times, is usually seeking recognition from others. Teachers often state that a child "is doing that *just* to get attention" as if gaining the attention of others is not something that we all desire at some level. Children whose needs for attention have not been met and who have had to resort to antics and rash behavior before being noticed, often struggle in a classroom where the teacher's attention is divided among many students. In our attempts to squelch the disruptive behavior, we must resist the inclination to ignore the student. More than anyone else, these children need our attention. We must make a concerted effort at "seeing," or engaging them and finding ways to validate them when they are not demanding our attention.

*We cannot possibly view life exactly as another person views life but, with careful attention and keen observation, we can discern how our students perceive life in our classrooms. Some students will be very transparent, using their own initiative to let us know who they are and in inviting us to become known to them. Getting to know students who are reticent requires more effort and patience on the teacher's part.*

One of the simplest ways to assure that we "see" students is to individually greet each student every day. The teacher might stand at the door as students enter or leave the class or perhaps the teacher may look up while calling the roll and greet each student personally. When a teacher vows to greet every student with a kind word, positive acknowledgment, a smile, the teacher does not do so with the idea that these behaviors will change the student, but with the assurance of changing oneself. When the teacher is changed, the students will change. When we come to a place where we find ourselves wanting to change another, we must look inside and see what it is that we can change within ourselves. For in fact, we are the only ones we can change. Exiled Vietnamese teacher and Buddhist monk, Thic Nhat

Hanh (1992) teaches that in coming to see another, we see ourselves. Part of you is me; part of me is you. When one of us feels separation, we all experience separation; when one of us experiences acceptance, we all feel acceptance. Living this philosophy in the classroom, teachers can quickly multiply the positive regard they feel for their students.

## Using our Childhood Memories

Each teacher has at some time or another spent time as a student. Yet, too often we forget to see life from the perspective of the student or of the child. The following is a story told to me by a friend whose memories of childhood had a direct bearing on how she dealt with one of her students. As a 9-year-old child attending boarding school in Africa, Anna accidentally dropped her spelling book into the outdoor toilet. Horrified, she ran to her older brother to retrieve it for her before someone else entered the toilet. In desperation, she drained scarce water from the storage tank to clean the book, sprinkled it with talcum powder and dried it in the sun. All these efforts only resulted in a very fat and smelly book. To Anna's astonishment, her teacher disgustedly threw the book into the trash but without so much as a single reprimand. Several weeks later, a new book appeared on Anna's desk.

Many years later, Anna allowed her students to take books home, admonishing that they were to take special precautions since the books were not hers. They were to put the books in their book bags but were not to put their lunches or any thermos in the same bag. One little girl disobeyed and the contents of her leaky thermos saturated the book. Anna, the teacher, was angry when she saw the ruined book, but before she responded to the child, she said, "Let me walk away a bit and think about this." She returned to her student and said, "I remember when I was 9, I did something even worse and my teacher simply gave me a new book. I won't punish you either. After all, it is only a book." Many valuable insights about how to respond to our students can be learned by recalling our own school experiences. In the incident above, a teacher recalls a kindness to guide her interaction. However, negative interactions can also serve to remind us what not to do.

Using our own lives as models for understanding our students has its limitations for we can never replicate the situations and contexts that our students are experiencing. Furthermore, we do not have the same temperaments and personalities as all of our students.

We cannot possibly view life exactly as another person views life but, with careful attention and keen observation, we can discern how our students perceive life in our classrooms. Some students will be very transparent, using their own initiative to let us know who they are and in inviting us to become known to them. Getting to know students who are reticent requires more effort and patience on the teacher's part.

Activities that help us get to know our students can be woven into almost any discipline. Disciplines that include the study of people, historical or fictional, can be used by asking our students to respond to a set of topics or questions relevant to the selected character. The students are asked to write as if they were that person using the first person singular pronoun, "I". We cannot talk about another without revealing something of ourselves. Yet, in assuming the role of another, we feel less vulnerable or exposed than when we are expressing our own views directly. Such assignments can be used to assess students' understanding of literature or history and, at the same time, demonstrate a student's ability to empathize and to take others' perspectives, essential skills for getting along with others.

## Building Trust

Teachers who want to get to know the students may ask students to tell about themselves through assignments or other activities designed to introduce individuals to the whole group. Too seldom, however, do teachers reciprocate by revealing stories or details of their own lives to their students. Students naturally want to know about the person who is the focus of much of their attention and who regularly impacts their lives. Recently, I attended a month-long seminar for college teachers. We met every day and were taught by two other college instructors. Over time, one instructor informally shared personal information in a context that related directly or indirectly to the course. His personal stories helped us to understand his perspective and lent credence to his knowledge of the subject. In contrast, the other instructor shared almost nothing of himself. Outside of class, I found myself with my fellow students constructing our own scenarios about his personal and professional background to fill in the gaps of what we had not been told. Students are simply curious. We can avoid speculations and misconceptions by being deliberate in what we disclose. We can also foster trust and openness by becoming real to our students.

Caroline Sinclair in *Looking for Home*, judiciously shares stories from her own life with her 11-year-old students, including mistakes that she made. She writes:

> We are in the company of people we trust where we can consider our ethics, confess our sins, admit our mistakes and still be taken back into the fold. We have seen that others have erred and we have forgiven them. What's more, we have seen ourselves in each other and in the actions of others. We are at home in each other's company and at home with ourselves. We are preparing to make our home in the world.

Sinclair (1994, p. 107)

By telling her own stories, she became vulnerable in ways that all students are vulnerable. As teachers we need not be fearful about disclosure; when we disclose information voluntarily, we satisfy students' need to connect and ground us to life outside the classroom. In the act of risking disclosure we become authentic, we are teachers who have become real people.

## Opportunities for Relating to Students

Stereotyping students can be reduced when a teacher takes the time to get to know something about each student. Teachers often use playground time and lunchtime as their own personal time and as a time to renew themselves amidst adult company. Teachers need these breaks, but occasionally spending time with students in small groups can be invaluable in seeing the students in a different context than the classroom. One teacher rewarded her 9- and 10-year-old students by eating lunch with them in small groups. The relaxed and informal atmosphere of the lunch period gave students and teacher a chance to talk to each other and to observe each other independent of the pressures of studies.

Depending on one's culture, inquiring about the personal welfare of another can take varied forms and is acceptable in varying degrees. Behind all of the social rules regarding expressions of respect is the larger and more important moral rule of respect as it is felt in the heart and soul of the individual. This is what we must pay attention to. In some cultures, one may be queried and advised by strangers regarding topics and in ways that other cultures might consider too personal and private for all but the very closest of confidants. I know of no place, however, where the art of listening, truly being present and attentive to another individual is considered rude or offensive. In the act of listening, the teller chooses what to reveal and to what degree. One of the most valuable gifts we can give our students is our undivided attention through listening. Simply listening is seeing another without judgment and trusting in the others' ability for transformation (Ueland, 1992).

## Helping Students Relate to Each Other

A primary grade teacher gathered her students around her to discuss what she deemed as an injustice toward a student who had repeated her class. Other students had begun to tease him and he was becoming agitated and angry. He was also showing signs of self-doubt and stress. The wise teacher put her arm around the student and began by telling a story of her own struggles as a young student. She shared with the children that she was nearly 14 when she finally learned to tell time, something that most of her 9-year-old students already knew how to do. She then verified that he had indeed repeated the class, a fact that other students were well aware of, and that he was making remarkable progress. This teacher did several things to restore the child's dignity. By acknowledging that her student had repeated the grade, she removed the power it had held as a dark secret. What everyone already knew was made public but in the context of the teacher's strong support and explanation. The child's dignity was restored—even his teacher had struggled, had lagged behind her classmates but had persevered.

Caring for students cannot and need not be overwhelming. To successfully care for and nurture others, we must acknowledge our own needs to be cared for. As adults we can assume that caring for ourselves is not indulgent, but essential if we are to have the energy and endurance to care for others over time.

## Creating a Safe Environment

A difficulty common among new teachers is finding the very intricate balance required to maintain order within a group and at the same time honoring student independence. Gaining students' respect for one's authority without demanding it overtly is something that successful, experienced teachers seem to do effortlessly. Part of the balance comes in having confidence in oneself—the other part is in respecting students enough to share the power. Shared power is not a negotiated truce—it comes from an internal sense of belonging to a world that is an ordered predictable place. The teacher establishes such an environment beginning with the very first introductions and expression of his or her expectations. The teacher takes the lead in setting conduct for students within the classroom and is the person in charge of making sure that the rules for civility and respect are carried out. When students realize that the teacher will uphold a standard that requires all students to abide by the same rules and that the teacher will deal with infractions equitably, students are likely to develop trust in the teacher. Trust in the teacher evokes a sense of security for the student. When the basic need of security is met, we are better able to take risks and perform more confidently.

In the discussion of caring and nurturing, the example described a teacher who contributed to the security of the whole group by standing by the student who was being taunted by his classmates. As teachers, we have many opportunities to teach fairness, acceptance and tolerance of others. In this case, students witnessed the teacher defending a child and reprimanding those who had teased him. She wisely did not stop there. She aligned herself with the child by revealing some of her own shortcomings. Because she responded to all injustices this way, she provided assurance to the whole class that were they ever to be the object of derision she, their teacher, would just as readily come to their defense. Furthermore, she was modeling empathy and understanding to the whole class.

Other teachers may have been just as adamantly opposed to the taunting and responded by extracting apologies from the children who were teasing. However, this teacher goes a step further. She takes the time to be sure that everyone understands the seriousness of the infraction and helps them to identify with the child being teased. She is still very much in charge but her response is not simply to power over the situation like a referee at a sporting event. What she does is the equivalent of peacemaker and diplomat and, of course, a caring teacher in charge of her classroom. When teachers take time to address relationship incidences in their classes, they are, in fact, claiming their right to teach students during their most teachable moments – moments linked with actual events. School curriculums may address issues of character and kindness at length, but it is those lessons that follow on the heels of lived-experience that will have the most impact on the student's consciousness and behavior.

## Expecting the Best

When a teacher upholds reasonably high expectations he or she gives students the message, "I believe that you are competent and able to do what I have asked." The research is clear, students perform at a level corresponding to reasonable expectations that teachers have for them (Rist, 1970). As teachers, we must ask ourselves, "Have I lowered my standards because of stereotypes? Have I categorized a whole group because the children are poor, because they and their families don't seem to care, because I think that they probably won't amount to much anyway, or because they have not done well in the past?" These kinds of beliefs hurt children by putting an artificial boundary between us (Martin & Cherian, 1999). We are no longer able to see them as individuals with whom to build relationships, rather they have become a group of stigmatized others.

When we view people from a deficit perspective, we are in danger of seeing only what they lack. William Ayers (1993) calls our penchant for labeling students as an upside down approach. By focusing on what children do not know, we neglect what they do know. In the area of classroom management, teachers can convey the message that "I expect that you will do the 'right' thing and that you will make decisions that will lead to good outcomes for you and for the class." Students who experience the teacher as being for them are less likely to cause trouble for the teacher or for other students.

*When teachers take time to address relationship incidences in their classes, they are, in fact, claiming their right to teach students during their most teachable moments—moments linked with actual events.*

By tapping in to the knowledge the teacher has of each student, the teacher can create situations that will help a particular child to become successful. One high school teacher, after learning that her student was homeless, shared her home and family with him. The student had been failing in school, but now that he had a safe place to sleep and a teacher who maintained high expectations, the student blossomed. This example far exceeds what most teachers can do or what most students need. However, creating situations that support students leads students to view the teacher as being on the "same team" as the students and not "out to get them". Holding consistently high expectations, with enthusiastic and organized support from the teacher, lead to student and teacher success.

# Conclusion

Our classes are situated in countries and in cultures that are as varied as we are. Certainly some of the ideas presented above are more viable for some situations than for others. This chapter is by no means an exhaustive set of considerations for the very complex world of human relationships, but it is hoped that the ideas presented above will perturb the reader to consider anew the power and responsibility that teachers have in co-creating relationships with their students—relationships that will enhance the well being of teachers and students alike. Teachers wield considerable power over the lives of their students and those who take their relationships with students seriously can impact students for good in lasting and immeasurable ways.

# References

Ayers, W. (1993). *To teach: The journey of a teacher.* New York: Teachers College Press.

Brazelton, T. B., & Greenspan, S.I. (2001). *The irreducible needs of children: What every child must have to grow, learn and flourish.* Cambridge, MA: Perseus Publications.

Bretherton, I., Ridgeway, D., & Cassidy, J. (1987). *The role of the internal working models in the attachment relationship.* Paper presented at the biennial meeting of the Society for Research in Child Development, Baltimore, MD.

Bretherton, I., & Waters, E. (1985). Attachment Theory: Retrospect and prospect. In I. Bretherton & E. Waters. (Eds.), *Growing points of attachment theory and research.* Monographs of the Society for Research in Child Development. 50(1-2), Serial No. 209, 3-38.

Collins, J. (1996). *The quiet child.* London: Cassell.

Hartup, W. W. (1989). Social Relationships and their developmental significance. *American Psychologist, 44,* 120-126.

Jernberg, A. M., (1981). *Theraplay.* San Francisco: Jossey-Bass Publishers.

Main, M., Kaplan, N., & Cassidy, J. (1985). Security in infancy, childhood and adulthood. In I. Bretherton & E. Waters. (Eds.), *Growing points of attachment theory and research.* Monographs of the Society for Research in Child Development, 50(1-2), Serial No. 209, 66-106.

Martin, D.M. (1991). *Preschool teacher-child relationships: An exploratory study of attachment models over time.* Unpublished dissertation. Virginia Polytechnic Institute and State University, VA.

Martin, D. M., & Cherian, M. (1999). Children, schools and social class. In V. Fu & A. Stremmel (Eds.), *Affirming diversity through democratic conversations* (pp. 105-123). Upper Saddle River, NJ: Merrill Press.

Pianta, R. (1999). *Enhancing relationships between children and teachers.* Washington, DC: American Psychological Association.

Rist, R. C. (1970). Student social class and teacher expectations: The self-fulfilling prophecy in ghetto education. *Harvard Educational Review, 4,* 411-451.

Sinclair, C. (1994). *Looking for home: A phenomenological study of home in the classroom.* New York: Suny Press.

Thich Nhat Hanh (1992). *Peace is every step.* New York: Bantam Books.

Ueland, B. (1992). Tell me more: On the fine art of listening. *Utne Reader,* Nov/Dec.1992 issue no. 54.

## About the Author

**Doris Martin,** Ph D, is an associate professor of Education at James Madison University in Virginia, U.S.A. Her first teaching experiences were with Head Start in Pennsylvania. During the next 12 years, she taught preschool and early grades and directed a laboratory school for children from infancy to age 10 in North Carolina. She has presented and published nationally on a wide range of topics including teacher-child relationships and the use of counselor- and teacher-led play therapy. Her current research focus is on the experiences of men as teachers in early childhood classrooms. Committed to deepening teachers' understanding of diverse socio-cultural contexts, Doris Martin conducted short-term education practica in Italy and Wales respectively for her student teachers from Virginia. In addition, she teaches Aikido, is an amateur potter and travels widely. E-mail: martindm@jmu.edu.

# CHAPTER 10

# Using Cooperative Learning in Large Classes

*George M. Jacobs & Loh Wan Inn*

"Our classrooms are too small." "It will waste a lot of time for students to get into groups." "How can we possibly monitor so many groups?" "A class of 50 students is hard enough to control already. Won't there be chaos if they start working in groups?" "Won't discipline suffer?" "The noise level will be too high." "Young children are too self-centered to work in groups." These are some concerns and questions we hear when we recommend group activities for large classes in Southeast Asia.

Southeast Asia is a very diverse region, with a wide variety of religions, languages, and ethnic groups represented, as well as great variance in terms of wealth, with per capita incomes ranging from less than US$1,000 a year to levels as high as those found in the world's wealthier countries. However, one thing the region does have in common is large class sizes. Even in relatively wealthy Singapore, 40 pupils per class is the norm. Classes of 50 and 60 are common in less well-to-do nations.

How do we respond when teachers express reservations about using group activities in their large classes? First, we acknowledge that larger classes make teaching more difficult and put a strain on teachers. We express the hope that soon the only place in school that large classes will be found is in the history books in the section about how school used to be before the situation improved. That said, we go on to express our belief that group activities, when organized according to concepts and techniques from cooperative learning, help us teachers cope better with large classes. This chapter describes how cooperative learning provides one means of making the best of facilitating learning in large classes.

# What is Cooperative Learning?

Cooperative learning can be defined as concepts and techniques for enhancing the value of student-student interaction. Cooperative learning has a long history going back at least to the 19th Century (Johnson & Johnson, 1999). Indeed, the ideas that "two (or more) heads are better than one" and that "many hands make light the work" have ancient roots in many of the world's cultures. In the Philippines, they call it the "Bayanihan spirit". In the Indonesian and Malay languages, it is called "gotong royong."

*When teaching large classes, we remind ourselves of the cooperative learning principle of Cooperation as a Value and imagine the world we are hoping to foster from within our classrooms. It is not a world in which people are controlled by the more powerful; it is a world in which people collaborate for the welfare of all.*

Slavin (1995) notes that a wide range of theories support the use of cooperative learning. Theories that underpin cooperative learning are supported by research (for reviews, see Johnson, Johnson & Stanne, 2000; Sharan, 1980; Slavin, 1995). Indeed, cooperative learning is perhaps the sub-field of education on which the most research has been done in many countries across all ages of students. What these studies show is that usually, but not always, group activities organized in line with cooperative learning principles lead to gains on an impressive variety of key variables in education, starting with gains in achievement as measured by standardized tests and other instruments. Other variables on which cooperative learning appears to have a positive impact include liking for school and for peers, self-esteem, locus of control (i.e., the idea that we have some control of our own fate), relations between different ethnic groups, acceptance of mainstreamed pupils, such as students with learning disabilities in the same class as other students, and thinking skills.

Here are a few examples of such studies. Slavin and Karweit (1984) compared the effects of cooperative learning and mastery learning on the mathematics achievement of secondary school students and found that those students who studied via cooperative learning outperformed those who used mastery learning. Calderon, Hertz-Lazarowitz, Ivory and Slavin (1997) found that when compared with other instructional methods, cooperative learning was generally associated with higher achievement in reading among primary school students enrolled in bilingual education programs.

As noted above, in addition to achievement, cooperative learning has also been associated with better results on affective measures. For instance, Johnson and Johnson (1981) conducted a study of friendships between handicapped and non-handicapped primary school students. They reported that when compared with individualistic learning experiences, working in cooperative learning groups promoted more cross-handicap friendships among students.

## Major Principles of Cooperative Learning

Different approaches to cooperative learning exist, each with a slightly different list of principles (Sharan, 1994, 2002; Slavin, 1995). Below are 8 principles we use in our own application of cooperative learning.

1. *Positive Interdependence* This principle lies at the heart of cooperative learning. This is what encourages group members to care about and support one another in the learning process. Positive interdependence represents the feeling among group members that they "sink or swim together," that what helps one member succeed helps all members succeed, and whatever hurts any group member, hurts all (Johnson & Johnson, 1999).

   Positive interdependence among group members can be encouraged in many ways. For instance, group members can have a common goal that they need to work together to achieve, such as understanding a mathematical procedure, answering a set of questions, preparing to do well on a quiz, or writing a letter. Another means of promoting positive interdependence is via a common identity, such as a group name or handshake. We can also divide resources that group members need to share in order to complete a task, such as when each group member has unique information. Additionally, there can be a common celebration or reward that groupmates will share if they achieve their goal, such as recognition from the teacher, performance of their silent team cheer, or bonus points. Further, each group member can play a different role in helping the group to function. Some of these rotating roles include timekeeper, encourager (who encourages everyone to participate), checker (who checks that everyone has understood), noise monitor (who reminds groupmates to use quiet voices), and recorder (who takes notes on what the group has discussed and decided).

2. *Individual Accountability*  Whereas positive interdependence involves group members supporting one another, individual accountability is about the pressure on each group member to learn and to help their groupmates learn. Individual accountability can be encouraged in many ways (Jacobs, Gan & Ball, 1997). For instance, each student can take a turn to tell their ideas to one or more groupmates. Alternatively, one at a time, students can write their ideas on a paper that circulates among the group. Another way to foster individual accountability is for each group member to take an individual quiz or hand in an individual assignment. Yet another way is for a teacher to randomly select a group member to report and explain to another group or to the class what their group thought or did.

3. *Heterogeneous Grouping*  Most approaches to cooperative learning recommend that students usually, but not always, work in heterogeneous groups (Cohen, 1994). An advantage is that students learn to work with people who are different from themselves. In that way, they are exposed to diverse ideas and perspectives from a variety of people. Heterogeneous groups may be formed using criteria such as past achievement, ethnicity, gender, first language, and personality (for instance, talkative-quiet, hardworking-relaxed).

4. *Collaborative Skills*  Rather than assume that students already have the skills needed to work together, teachers provide explicit instruction and structured practice in these collaborative skills (Johnson & Johnson, 1999). Also, the class discusses the importance of such skills. Many collaborative skills play key roles in effective group function. These include asking for help, providing reasons, disagreeing politely, checking that others understand, using quiet voices, listening attentively, and taking turns.

5. *Equal Participation*  A common problem in groups is that some group members end up doing most of the work and, as a result,

most of the learning. Cooperative learning seeks to address this by attempting to structure the interaction in the groups so as to make the participation more equal (Kagan, 1994). Cooperative learning seeks to encourage equal participation in a number of ways.

First, in some techniques no one speaks or writes twice until everyone in the group has spoken or written once. Another means is for students to have rotating roles in the group (for example, first they are the interviewer and then they are the interviewee). A third means is for each student to be given a set amount of time to share their ideas with one or more group mates. Also, groups do not have a permanent representative who always speaks for the group. Instead, everyone gets a chance to play that role.

6. *Simultaneous Interaction* This principle provides a central rationale for the use of groups, particularly in large classes. In the typical teacher-fronted classroom, the interaction pattern is sequential interaction. In other words, one person talks at a time. The classic pattern of sequential interaction involves teacher talk, then teacher nomination of individual students to talk (often to answer a question by the teacher), student response, and teacher evaluation of the student's response. In this interaction format, each student has very little opportunity to talk. This is particularly the case in large classes.

Group activities radically alter this one-at-a-time scenario, because instead of one person per class talking, now one person per group is talking simultaneously, hence the term "simultaneous interaction" (Kagan, 1994). Thus, if a class of 48 students is working in foursomes, 12 students (1 in each group of 4) are talking at the same time. If the class is working in pairs, 24 are talking simultaneously. The principle of simultaneous interaction is one reason for keeping groups small. With 8 students per group in our class of 48, only 6 students are talking simultaneously during group activities.

7. *Group Autonomy* For many people—students, administrators, parents and teachers—teaching means the teacher talking. So, what are we teachers supposed to do when our students are working in groups? What we should not do is to jump in and take over a group the first time students face difficulty. Instead, we should encourage groups to solve their own problems. We want

to shift some of the power about what happens in the classroom and some of the responsibility for learning and behavior away from ourselves and give it to students in their groups (Baloche, 1998; Cohen, 1994).

By encouraging groups to feel more autonomous from their teachers, we are not abandoning students. We are not giving them a task to do cooperatively and then heading to the school canteen for a glass of mango juice or burying ourselves at our desks to catch up on marking. Instead, we are walking around monitoring the groups to see how well they understand concepts, how well they perform skills, and how well they work together. Sometimes, we intervene to help the groups function more effectively, but other times we do not.

8. **Cooperation as a Value**   Last, but definitely not least, comes the idea that cooperation represents not only a way to learn but also a value to appreciate and to incorporate in all aspects of our lives (Forest, 2001; Sapon-Shevin, 1999). This does not mean that competition should be banned or that students should never work alone. However, in much of today's world, cooperation is devalued and unappreciated (Kohn, 1992).

By making cooperation a value, we broaden the concept of cooperation beyond what happens in small groups of 2, 3 or 4 students. We extend the concept by encouraging students to recognize and act upon the positive interdependence that exists between themselves and others throughout the class, throughout the school, throughout their community, throughout their country, and around the world, including not just humans but other species as well. We can use many ways to promote cooperation as a value and enhance the positive interdependence of our actions on the lives of all around us.

For instance, groups can each do an aspect of a class project. Additionally, class and school goals can be used rather than only group goals. When these goals are achieved, class or school celebrations can be held or other rewards can be given. Cooperation can extend beyond the school as well. For example, students can be involved in projects outside the school to help others and to protect the environment. Along the same lines, communication and joint tasks can be carried out with students from different schools in the same country and internationally.

Examination of these cooperative learning principles clearly shows the difference between cooperative learning and traditional group work. In traditional group work, we ask students to form groups and hope that everything will go well. With cooperative learning, we plan, prepare, and follow-up in order to give the group activities the best possible opportunity to succeed. Part of this planning and preparation involves drawing upon cooperative learning principles, as well as sharing ideas with other educators by discussing and examining the literature on cooperative learning.

## Four Cooperative Learning Techniques

There are over 100 different cooperative learning techniques that can be used in any subject area and with any age of student. What we do is to take a cooperative learning technique, add some content, and we have a cooperative learning activity (Kagan, 1994). These four techniques have been selected because they are simple to use and do not involve students moving from one group to another. The examples given along with each technique have been taken from elementary school so that they are understandable to all readers of this chapter, but, as stated above, the techniques can be used with all ages of learners, including adults.

*RallyRobin* (Kagan, 1994)   This technique is done in pairs. Person #1 gives an idea; #2 gives another idea and #1 gives yet another idea, etc. The teacher calls a number and then selects a few students with that number (not every student with that number) to share their partner's idea with the class.

a. Examples
- ◆ General: #1 answers Question #1 in a textbook exercise, #2 answers Question #2, #1 answers Question #3, etc.
- ◆ Mathematics (multiplication): #1 says "1 x 5 = 5," #2 says "2 x 5 = 10," #1 says "3 x 5 = 15," etc.
- ◆ Science (plant parts): #2 says "stem" and describes its function; #1 says "roots" and describes their function, #2 says "flowers" and describes their function, etc.

b. A variation is RallyTable (Kagan, 1994) which is the same, except that students write instead of speaking, passing a piece of paper between them.

*Review Pairs* (Johnson & Johnson, 1991)   Groups of 4 begin as two pairs, each working with the same set of problems or questions. Person #1 (the Thinker) in the pair reads aloud the first problem/question and thinks aloud as they work on it. Person #2 (the Coach) listens, watches, and coaches. This coaching involves suggestions, encouragement, and questions, but it does not involve doing the work for the partner. Partners exchange the roles of Thinker and Coach for each subsequent problem/question. After every two problems/questions, the two pairs in the foursome get together to discuss their responses and try to reach consensus about possible answers. After the discussion, they thank each other for their ideas and continue with the next two problems/questions.

Examples
♦ Language Arts: The questions that appear after a reading passage can be used.
♦ Social Studies: Students can think aloud about hypothetical situations that involve changes to the current situation, e.g., How would the place we live in be different if no one had cars?

*Question-and-Answer Pairs* (Johnson & Johnson, 1991)   In this technique, each member of a pair writes questions/problems. These questions can involve only retrieval of information already covered, or the questions can involve higher order thinking. Then, students write answers to their own questions. Next, students trade questions, answer each other's questions (providing support for their answers), and then compare answers.

Examples
♦ Mathematics: Students write problems that are similar to the ones in their textbook. In their answers, they show the steps involved in solving the problems.
♦ Science: After finishing a chapter on water in their textbook, students write multiple choice and open-ended questions to trade with their partners.

*Numbered Heads Together* (Kagan, 1994)   In this technique, each member of a group has a number, for instance, 1, 2, 3 or 4 if students are in foursomes. The teacher asks a question and group members literally and figuratively put their heads together to develop an answer to the question and reasons to support their answer. Then, the teacher calls a number (1, 2, 3 or 4) at random. Students with that number give and explain their group's answer.

Examples
♦ General: The teacher can use the questions in the textbook or workbook.
♦ Language Arts: The teacher can give students sentences with grammar errors. Students need to find the error, say why it is an error, and redo the sentence in a correct form.
♦ Science: Students put their heads together to plan an investigation to answer a question.

## Why Use Cooperative Learning in Large Classes?

Now, let us return to the specific case of cooperative learning in large classes. Is cooperative learning more difficult in large classes? Yes, but so is any type of teaching. The point, however, is that the problem of large classes makes cooperative learning even more necessary than it is in smaller classes. Here are three reasons why cooperative learning is particularly useful in large classes.

First, in a teacher-fronted mode of instruction, the larger the class, the less each student gets to speak. As mentioned in the principle of Simultaneous Interaction, cooperative learning helps students become more active. The talking that students do in groups pushes them to understand better so as to be able to put their understanding into words. Second, in large classes, it is difficult for teachers to provide much feedback to individual students. In contrast, with cooperative learning, group mates are right there to supply feedback. Third, in large classes, students may easily feel lost and anonymous. However, with cooperative learning, each person is part of a group that cares about whether they are present and how they are doing.

## The Details of Using Cooperative Learning in Large Classes

As mentioned earlier, cooperative learning requires planning, preparation and follow-up. In this part of the chapter, we share detailed ideas for dealing with the issues raised in the opening paragraph of this chapter. These ideas come from our discussions with teachers in Southeast Asia, our observation of their classes, our own teaching, and books on cooperative learning (Jacobs, Power & Loh, 2002).

## "Our classrooms are too small."

With 25 students in a normal-sized classroom, arranging the seating for cooperative learning poses few difficulties. However, with a lot of students in a cramped classroom, careful planning is needed so that the seating works. Here are some pointers.

(1) Students should sit close to one another. This facilitates the sharing of materials, the use of quiet voices that do not disturb other groups (e.g., "15 cm voices"—ones that can only be heard 15 centimetres away), and a feeling among group mates that they are, indeed, part of a group. (2) The seating arrangement should allow space for us to walk around the room and monitor all the groups. (3) Keeping group size small, 4 or less, makes it easier to arrange the seating. In fact, pairs are probably the easiest size to arrange. Big groups make individual accountability and equal participation more difficult, because individuals are more likely to avoid responsibility or be left out in a large group. (4) A uniform arrangement for all groups is preferred. Each pupil has a number in their group, e.g., 1, 2, 3, or 4, with all the #1s seated in the same place in their groups. In this way, students and teachers know who in each group has which number.

## "It will waste a lot of time for students to get into groups."

We have seen students take 5 or more noisy, chaotic minutes to arrange themselves into their groups. Here are some things we can do to avoid this. Firstly, students should be in the same group for at least 5 weeks. As noted above, these should be heterogeneous groups. When students stay in the same group for such a length of time, they immediately know whom they should be sitting with. Also, students have time to build a feeling of positive interdependence with their group mates.

*Is cooperative learning more difficult in large classes? Yes, but so is any type of teaching. The point, however, is that the problem of large classes makes cooperative learning even more necessary than it is in smaller classes.*

Secondly, if possible, students should sit with their group mates all the time and desks should be arranged so that students are already sitting in groups whether or not they are working as a group. In this way, no moving is necessary. Thirdly, if movement is necessary, the class should practice moving quickly and quietly into groups. Finally, if chairs or desks, not just students, need to move, tape or other kinds of marking on the floor can make this easier.

## *"How can we possibly monitor so many groups?"*

Another disadvantage of large classes is that teachers have more students to monitor. As stated previously in regard to the principle of group autonomy, cooperative learning reduces this burden a bit because peers, not just teachers, are doing the monitoring. Here are some ideas on how we can observe groups.

After an activity has begun, we can make a quick tour to check that all the groups seem to be on track. Later, we can focus on a particular group that experience tells us is likely to have more difficulties than most. If that group seems to be doing well, probably most other groups are also doing well. On the other hand, we may want to spend some time with one of the groups that seems to be doing particularly well. That group may be using strategies that we can pass on to the rest of the class. If groups call on us for assistance, we can use the TTT policy. TTT means Team Then Teacher. In other words, students should first turn to their group mates for help. We teachers come into the picture only if the group cannot help. TTT fits with the principle of group autonomy.

## *"A class of 50 students is hard enough to control already. Won't there be chaos if they start working in groups?"*

One of the agreeable things about teaching is that every day is full of surprises. One of the disagreeable things about teaching is that not all those surprises are pleasant. Lessons go wrong, even lessons that have worked beautifully in the past. With a small class, we can quickly go around to each group and repair the damage. This is much more difficult with a large class. Thus, we need to try to give very clear directions. Here are a few suggestions for doing that.

We need to have everyone's attention before giving directions. One way to do this is by an attention signal. A popular attention signal is RSPA. It works like this. The teacher claps and raises a hand.

Upon hearing and/or seeing this, students **R**aise their hand. When they raise their hand, they **S**top talking at the end of the sentence they are speaking. Students **P**ass the signal to groups/classmates who have not heard/seen it. Finally, students give their **A**ttention to the teacher or whoever else has given the signal.

Another key to successful lessons in large classes using cooperative learning is for students to understand the objectives of the lesson, how a particular task fits into the overall plan for the course, and how their work will be evaluated. With this understanding, the directions will make more sense to students, and they will have a clearer purpose for following them.

Instructions should be written where students can refer to them, such as on an OHT, data projector, or blackboard. We might want to give the instructions step by step, rather than all at once. Also, we can demonstrate how to do the activity, with students as our group mates, or a group of students can demonstrate. As a further check, before students begin the activity, we can ask a member of the class to repeat the procedure to the whole class and/or ask a member of each group to repeat it to their group mates. Yet another idea is for one student per group to act as a facilitator who is responsible for their group working efficiently. At the same time that we try to make directions clear, we may also want to be flexible about how the activity is done, either by asking students for their suggestions or by letting them change the instructions as they go along.

## "Won't discipline suffer?"

Discipline is an important factor in learning. The potential for discipline problems is greater in larger classes. Here are some ideas how cooperative learning can aid, rather than impede classroom discipline.

Because group activities add a social element to learning and provide students with a better chance to succeed (thanks to help from peers), students may enjoy class more and be more on-task. We also need to examine the tasks we use: they should be do-able, as frustration can lead to misbehavior; and they should be interesting, as boredom can lead to misbehavior.

Additionally, group activities give students more responsibility for what happens in class. Hopefully, they will exercise that responsibility wisely. This responsibility sharing can be achieved by involving students in formulating and enforcing class policies on how to behave during group activities. Such policies might include everyone having a chance to participate, everyone helping others understand, everyone asking for help when needed, everyone speaking in quiet voices, everyone following the Attention Signal.

## *"The noise level will be too high."*

One of the great things about group activities is that they give students many opportunities to talk as they brainstorm, plan, share ideas, explain, debate, question, and summarize. However, in the case of large classes, the more students in the class, the more voices there are. The more voices there are, the higher the noise level can become. Here are some ideas for achieving a noise level that, as Robert Slavin (1995) states, should sound like a beehive, not a sports event.

We can explain to students why the sound level should be kept down. At the same time, we can tolerate a somewhat higher sound level in return for having students be more active. Additionally, students can learn to use two different voices: a 15-cm voice in their groups (discussed above); and a class-size voice when they are speaking to the entire class.

The way students are seated can also affect the sound level. The smaller the groups and the closer together the group members are sitting, the smaller the distance their voices need to travel to be heard by their group mates. Further, one group member can act as a Noise Monitor. This is another means of sharing responsibility with students.

In addition to an attention signal, such as RSPA, we can have another signal that says, "Please continue discussing, but do so more quietly." Last, but not least, the quietest way for students to work together is by writing. Many cooperative learning techniques, e.g., RallyTable described earlier in this chapter, involve writing in addition to or instead of speaking. This writing can be done on paper or with a computer.

## *"Young children are too self-centered to work in groups."*

Some teachers express reservations about using group activities with large classes of very young children. The characteristics of young children such as self-centeredness and impulsiveness are seen as factors that make group work difficult. As teachers, we should be facilitating children in their development of their self-concept. Group work based on the principles of cooperative learning, such as positive interdependence, helps us nurture young children's sense of identity, belonging, and acceptance by fostering care and support for one another rather than undue focus on the self. Further, the need to collaborate with peers provides a venue for young children to practice restraint.

With young children especially, it is better to start off with pair work, moving to work in slightly larger groups when they have improved their collaborative skills. Pairs can do such tasks as working on a shared puzzle with each child holding different pieces of the puzzle, dressing a doll with each child taking turns, or working on a collage with each child making contributions. Such cooperative work teaches children to consider another person's viewpoint while nurturing their own self-confidence.

## Conclusion

In this chapter, we began with a brief introduction to cooperative learning. Next, we looked at why cooperative learning should be used in large classes and made some suggestions for how this can be achieved. We have only skimmed the surface in this chapter, as the facilitation of student-student interaction is a huge topic. Fortunately, a large body of literature now exists on cooperative learning. The reference list below offers an entry point into that literature.

Faced with the difficulties that large classes can pose, teachers' first reaction may be to resort to methods of control that utilize our power over students. The authors of this chapter have at times succumbed to this temptation. Happily, what we have learned about cooperative learning provided us with better ways of dealing with large classes. When teaching large classes, we remind ourselves of the cooperative learning principle of Cooperation as a Value and imagine the world we are hoping to foster from within our classrooms. It is not a world in which people are controlled by the more powerful; it is a world in which people collaborate for the welfare of all. Toward this goal, we urge you, the readers of our chapter, to try cooperative learning in your classes large and small.

## References

Baloche, L. (1998). *The cooperative classroom: Empowering learning.* Upper Saddle River, NJ: Prentice Hall.

Calderón, M., Hertz-Lazarowitz, R., Ivory, G., & Slavin, R. E. (1997). *Effects of bilingual cooperative integrated reading and composition on students transitioning from Spanish to English reading.* Report No. 10. Center for Research on the Education of Students Placed at Risk, Johns Hopkins University & Howard University. ERIC Document Reproduction Service No. ED 405 428

Cohen, E. (1994). *Designing groupwork: Strategies for the heterogeneous classroom* (2nd ed.). New York: Teachers College Press.

Forest, L. (2001). *Crafting creative community: Combining cooperative learning, multiple intelligences, and nature's wisdom.* San Clemente, CA: Kagan.

Jacobs, G. M., Gan S. L., & Ball, J. (1997). *Learning cooperative learning via cooperative learning: A sourcebook of lesson plans for teacher education.* San Clemente, CA: Kagan Publications and Professional Development.

Jacobs, G. M., Power, M. A., & Loh W. I. (2002). *The teachers' sourcebook for cooperative/collaborative learning.* Thousand Oaks, CA: Corwin.

Johnson, D. W., & Johnson, R. T. (1991). *Cooperative learning lesson structures.* Edina, MN: Interaction Book Company.

Johnson, D. W., & Johnson, R. T. (1999). *Learning together and alone: Cooperative, competitive, and individualistic learning* (5th ed.). Boston, MA: Allyn and Bacon.

Johnson, D. W., Johnson, R. T., & Stanne, M.B. (2000). *Cooperative learning methods: A meta-analysis.* Retrieved July, 2000 from http://www.clcrc.com/pages/cl-methods.html.

Johnson, R. T., & Johnson, D. W. (1981). Building friendships between handicapped and non-handicapped students: Effects of cooperative and individualistic instructiiton. *American Educational Research Journal, 18*, 415-424.

Kagan, S. (1994). *Cooperative learning.* San Clemente, CA: Kagan Publications and Professional Development.

Kohn, A. (1992). *No contest: The case against competition.* (2nd ed.). Boston: Houghton Miflin.

Sapon-Shevin, M. (1999). *Because we can change the world: A practical guide to building cooperative, inclusive classroom communities.* Boston, MA: Allyn and Bacon.

Sharan, S. (1980). Cooperative learning in small groups: Recent methods and effects on achievement, attitudes and ethnic relations. *Review of Educational Research, 50*, 241-271.

Sharan, S.. (Ed.). (1994). *Handbook of cooperative learning methods.* Westport, CN: Greenwood Press.

Sharan, S. (2002). Differentiating methods of cooperative learning in research and practice. *Asia Pacific Journal of Education. 22*, 106-116.

Slavin, R. E. (1995). *Cooperative learning: Theory, research, and practice* (2nd ed.). Englewood Cliffs, NJ: Prentice Hall.

Slavin, R. E., & Karweit, N. (1984). Mastery learning and student teams: A factorial experiment in urban general mathematics classes. *American Educational Research Journal, 21,* 725-736.

## About the Authors

**George Jacobs** is an education consultant (www.georgejacobs.net). He has taught in Central America, China, Thailand, and the United States. From 1993-2000, he was a language specialist at the Southeast Asia Ministers of Education Organization's Regional Language Centre, Singapore. He serves on the executive board of the International Association for the Study of Cooperation in Education (www.iasce.net) and edits the newsletter of the TESOLers for Social Responsibility caucus of Teachers of English to Speakers of Other Languages (www.tesolers4sr.org). He and Loh Wan Inn are currently completing a book on cooperative learning to be published by Corwin Press (www.corwinpress.com). E-mail: gmjacobs@pacific. net.sg.

**Loh Wan Inn** is an education consultant. She has lived and worked in the U.S., Singapore, Ireland and Australia. Her first teaching experiences were with the National Institute of Education, Singapore. Over the years, she has conducted workshops and courses for teachers in science education from preschool to secondary levels. She was involved in teacher training and has designed and conducted camps on multiple intelligences and science for teachers. E-mail: wiloh@singnet.com.sg.

# CHAPTER 11

# Getting to Know Every Student through Portfolios

*Rosalind Y. Mau*

I invited my large class of students to a buffet of hot spicy noodles, chicken, mixed green salad, fruit and cakes. Some relished all the food while others were more picky. When some parents asked me what their children ate, I said, "The students ate the food and seemed to enjoy themselves." I could not give more definitive answers in terms of food students liked best, how much they ate or whether they were satisfied.

Similarly, students in large classes are often seen as a whole. Individual students who are noticed and remembered tend to be those who do very well, those who perform poorly and those who are challenging in some way or another. Students in between these extremes may be neglected. Teachers who wish to get to know every child may find using individual student portfolios effective. A portfolio captures, in one place, a student's interests, progress and attitudes toward different activities. Besides informing teachers, portfolios engage students in their learning and may be used during parent conferences. Portfolios for large classes do require an investment of time and energy. Teachers might wonder if portfolios are worth the effort of gathering, processing and reflecting on learning experiences. I am confident that teachers will see the value once they begin to use the portfolio to improve their teaching and increase student learning.

## What are Portfolios?

Portfolios are purposeful collections of a student's effort, progress and achievement over time. A collection may include: samples of work—for example, writing samples, art pieces—selected by the student based on what the student wishes to show about himself or herself; the student's reflections as self assessment is done and connections are made with what is learnt and what is meaningful; items such as tests following the teacher's guidelines and criteria for judging what strong performance is.

Portfolios can take the form of a folder to keep project-work material or electronic files on a computer. As projects develop over time, portfolios with observations and reflections document stages of learning and dispositions. This leads to a more accurate picture of student learning than a group test at the end of a project.

*As teachers systematically collect authentic work through portfolios, they capture the effectiveness of active and engaged learning by students as well as meet accountability standards for the school. So teachers of large classes have a better understanding of each student through portfolios.*

More recently, electronic portfolios have gained popularity because they conveniently communicate student progress to parents, teachers and students themselves. Use of an electronic portfolio provides a space for students to have collaborative exchanges when they are not in the classroom. It creates conditions that allow students to find different channels of support. This allows students to learn anywhere, anytime and at their own pace with others. Electronic portfolios capture working drafts of a paper, digitized pictures of work, video, and completed assessments. For more information, see a website at http://electronicportfolios.com.

## Purposes of Portfolios

A common purpose of portfolios is to showcase the best work of students. Portfolios that capture the best work of primary/elementary students include core and individualized items. Core items are based on key curriculum objectives. In primary school, the domains cover the whole curriculum such as language, mathematics, science, social studies and the arts. In secondary school, the domains are within a specific content area of, for instance, science or across several subject areas in interdisciplinary work. Core items are designed to show growth over time and the quality of work across the curriculum. Individualized items represent an area of special interest to a student or a significant event of learning. They are designed to portray the unique characteristics of students and to reflect their work in a specific domain.

A second purpose of portfolios is to document student learning over a period of time. An example is Gardner's (1991) *processfolio* where students observe, record and provide evidence of their planning and implementing of projects. Content choices vary to match different learning experiences. Teachers specify contents ranging from highly structured to unstructured. A highly structured item is a journal entry on a particular topic. Moderately structured items are many drafts of a writing process, a multimedia project or a research report. Loosely structured contents are written work over a month or by subject area. Lastly, unstructured contents are whatever students wish to include in their portfolio. This approach of gathering a variety of content items is compatible with today's understanding of the variability in how students think and learn.

A third purpose is for accountability to stakeholders. For example, parents can sift through and discuss the portfolio material with teachers. They are able to examine student progress and ask pertinent questions to teachers during parent-teacher conferences. Students themselves are held accountable as they become more aware of what they are learning and have clear guidelines of how to complete their portfolios. As stakeholders, teachers use portfolios to assess and grade students for accountability purposes.

## Assessment of Portfolios

Portfolios integrate learning and authentic assessment by providing continuous information on how students are doing. In this way, students are encouraged to observe their own progress as they receive teacher feedback. Scoring of these portfolios record achievement during the learning process. Students may include a baseline assessment or initial draft of a paper, samples of work, and assessment tools that guide and monitor students' work. Assessment tools, such as checklists and rating scales, are completed by teachers, by peer-classmates or by students themselves.

*Checklists and Rating Scales*   A checklist is used to see whether something is present or not. Teachers use an observation checklist to record what students are expected to know and do. They mark "yes" or "no" on a checklist when evaluating whether a piece of work is organized or has met a criterion of neatness. Used in combination with anecdotal records and samples of student work, teachers use the checklist to document student development. In this way, teachers guide students toward challenging experiences rather than to those they have already mastered or they are not ready to attempt. A rating scale is similar to a checklist. Rather than a checklist with two choices, a rating scale has three or more choices. For example, for an item reading "Is a piece of work organized?", the choices could be "well-organized", "somewhat organized" or "not organized". Commonly used choices for criteria are "not yet", "is learning" and "proficient" or "emergent", "beginning", "developing" and "fluent".

A Work Sampling approach (Helm, Beneke & Steinheimer, 1998) uses rating scales to assess and document knowledge, skills and accomplishments across multiple occasions. This approach helps teachers understand how to observe, collect and analyze student work. Observation rating scales show levels of behavior as students work on a project or learn a task. Teachers use rating scales with scoring rubrics to evaluate student products such as research papers, models of things or oral presentations.

Portfolios of the best work of students also are assessed by teachers and by the students themselves using rating scales and clearly written rubrics. Figure 1 is an example of a rating scale with rubrics completed by students when they turn in their portfolios:

## Figure 1: A Student's Self-rating Scale of Portfolios

|  | Approaching expectation | Meeting expectation | Exceeding expectation |
|---|---|---|---|
| I included a reflection for each piece of work in the portfolio | missing a reflection | a reflection for each piece | all reflections well-done |
| I organized my portfolio with care | poorly organized | is organized | is very well organized |
| I am satisfied with my portfolio | needs some improvement | satisfied | extremely satisfied |

In addition, teachers may ask students to write comments at the end of the rating scale under sections such as "I have improved in these areas" and "I need improvement in these areas".

**Reflections**   Another assessment tool used in portfolios is self or group reflections that range from short-project summaries to learning logs written on a daily basis. Whatever the length, reflections are valuable in capturing students' development of knowledge, skills and dispositions.

***Concept Maps*** Yet another assessment tool is a learning web or concept map. Students may submit many pieces of work in a portfolio and link them with a learning web. Students submit concept maps to document their learning and help them visualize the relationship between concepts and categories of learning. A comparison of an initial concept web and a final web may show growth of knowledge and thinking over the course of the project. Teachers may see the new vocabulary and informational relationship between words and concepts. For example, for a project on Transportation, a student's initial concept web may have first level connections with "car", "train", "plane", "motorcycle", "van" and "rocket". The final concept web may have more levels of connections for "transportation": (1) "by air" may branch into "rocket", "jet plane" and "hot air balloon"; (2) "by land" may branch into "van", "truck", "foot mobile", "motorcycle", "car" and "bus"; and (3) "by water" into "boat", "ship", "jet ski", "surfboard", "seaplane" and "aircraft carrier".

***Summary*** Assessment of student portfolios measures progress of learning and achievement of learning targets. Teachers of large classes can vary their assessment tools to match learning experiences and to meet different student modes of learning. Paper and pencil tests, checklists and rating scales are tools used to see if curriculum objectives are met. In addition, self-reflections, learning journals and concept maps are in portfolios so students can assess themselves and make connections about what they learn and what is meaningful to them. As teachers systematically collect authentic work through portfolios, they capture the effectiveness of active and engaged learning by students as well as meet accountability standards for the school. So teachers of large classes have a better understanding of each student through portfolios.

# Benefits of Using Portfolios

***Portfolios Capture Quality of Thinking and Work*** While students put together a portfolio, they see themselves as learners over a period of time. Learning is related to feelings about learning (Howard, 1994). How students feel about learning and whether they want to learn have a long-range effect on achievement. Students' words in learning journals often reveal their dispositions toward learning. For instance, an entry might read: "I feel good about working with Harry because he shares his inner convictions with me and leads me to clarify what I think." Teachers pay attention to "I statements" in order to consciously develop a way of understanding students. Besides reading student reflections in logs, teacher observations recorded on rating scales along with anecdotal notes enhance a teacher's perception of students' emotional responses and dispositions to learning.

Students become aware of engaged and meaningful learning when they construct their own knowledge from compiling a portfolio. When students complete assessment forms with clear criteria and rubrics, they learn to gauge their own progress and develop ways to best complete an assignment. Gathering evidence in a portfolio concentrates the mind on the learning process and how it might be improved. Types of evidence are simple statements of what has been learned (concepts and underlying principles, checklist of activities done) and reflections including opinions on how meaningful and relevant their learning has been.

*Good decisions are based on the accuracy, reliability and relevance of the evidence that is collected in portfolios. By documenting students' work, teachers know what knowledge and skills students have and when to introduce a new concept or skill.*

Portfolios can capture change and development over time. An authentic learning process begins with and values the meanings that students attribute to specific events. They are encouraged to use divergent and creative thinking patterns to process viable options. As they summarize and converge on an idea, this may lead to "satisficing" as opposed to "optimising" the number of options (Perkins & Blythe, 1994). A search for alternatives involve *sufficient* search for possibilities and *fairness* in the search of evidence. In evaluating all options, students try to find common areas from multiple frames of reference and to accommodate diverse patterns of thinking. Thinking is directed by portfolio objectives that provide the essential direction and possibilities.

In contrast to structured tests, portfolios capture a richer array of what students know and can do. Knowledge, skills and dispositions for life-long learning are promoted in portfolios. Students learn to make decisions on material for inclusion into their portfolio. They monitor their own learning so they can adjust and do what is necessary to complete, for instance, a project. Learning using portfolios goes beyond knowledge of facts to problem solving, from recall to critical and creative thinking and from passive to active, more confident learners.

***Portfolios Inform about Students' Learning***   Teachers use supporting information from portfolios to plan curriculum based on the students' level of development. The earlier example of the "Transportation" concept maps before and after learning illustrates this. Teachers—whether they teach small or large classes—must perceive how students learn to help them develop. Portfolios enable teachers to see learning through analyzing what has been placed in individual portfolios. Rather than focus on deficits, portfolios identify student strengths and monitor progress. Documentation of student work through portfolios is a basis for adjusting teaching strategies. Teachers can see through careful and systematic recording of learning how students are solving problems, working together and developing social dispositions. Moreover, portfolios provide evidence that supports teachers in making decisions. Good decisions are based on the accuracy, reliability and relevance of the evidence that is collected in portfolios. By documenting students' work, teachers know what knowledge and skills students have and when to introduce a new concept or skill.

***Portfolios Facilitate Communication***   Portfolios serve as a medium for discussion between students and their teachers, students with other students and parents with teachers. They are useful for communication because they record student progress over time, are detailed and complex records of learning, and show what students think through reflections. Portfolios are successful tools for communication when they have a sharp focus on the purpose of the portfolio. Is it to record best work, progress of learning, process and product of a project or is it a status report?

Teachers communicate their expectations to students by delineating clear and authentic achievement targets that are held steady and made explicit. Clear and valid criteria in evaluating portfolios require checklists and rating scales. Quality communication depends on specificity, which means supportive examples of learning, integration of important concepts and new insights for future learning (Stiggins, 1997).

## Putting Together a Portfolio

*Stage 1: Identify Goals and Context*  Purposes for portfolios vary broadly from instruction in one subject area to over several disciplines as in project work and to classroom assessment. Some specific purposes are to show growth or change over time, to create collections of personally important work and to prepare a sample of best work. Other purposes are to trace the evolution of a project and to review curriculum or instruction.

Teachers start with curriculum goals and objectives. In this way, teachers more effectively align their teaching with the school-level curriculum. Afterward, they think about the activities and assessment to best provide evidence of achievement of these goals and objectives. For example, if the objective is to select a topic for writing, the teacher could have a checklist of items such as: "student has looked at three sources for an idea"; "has provided a list of advantages and disadvantages for topic choice"; and "has reflected on reasons for selecting a particular topic".

To be accountable to school goals, teachers develop their lesson plans from curriculum objectives. While they may teach knowledge, skills and dispositions in various ways, the teachers focus on these objectives.

*Stage 2: Collection and Storage*  A meaningful learning environment for large classes begins with and values what students attribute to their own learning. Prepare students to select and collect their own portfolio items. Take the time to teach them how to do learning webs or concept maps, checklists or rating scales, and reflections. Students learn that reflections provide them the opportunity to look at and make sense of their experiences, see the changes and develop a sense of achievement.

*Portfolios often have been treated as a container to hold the work of students. As a result of this container approach, portfolios have no consistency across students. With large classes, the consistency becomes critical. Standardising the portfolio format helps.*

Tell students to select representative material which meet criteria set by the teacher. Encourage students to interject their personality in deciding what to include and how to store their portfolio. Provide conditions where students approach problems and solutions in multiple ways that do not constrain their methods of analysis and production to a single way.

***Stage 3: Reflection*** Think and decide why material was selected by indicating the meaning and value to the learner. Students should be encouraged to document reasons for selecting items to be included in the portfolio. The portfolio can include a reflective learning journal with a format that has reflections on the each of the items using stems such as:

**(1)** "This item was a great challenge to me because…";

**(2)** "I found this item meaningful because…"; and

**(3)** "I feel I can apply what I have learned from this item because…".

***Stage 4: Organisation and Presentation*** The following are guidelines for teachers to consider.

- When introducing the portfolio, give students a handout with clear instructions and criteria for marking, and show examples of portfolios.
- Develop protocols such as a time schedule with specific dates for completion of various portfolio parts.
- Plan for individual and group conferences during class time when students are working on their portfolios.

## Standardising the Portfolio for Large Classes

Portfolios often have been treated as a container to hold the work of students. As a result of this container approach, portfolios have no consistency across students. With large classes, the consistency becomes critical. Standardising the portfolio format helps. I recommend having four key components: a thesis statement, pieces of evidence, descriptions and analysis of that evidence, and a conclusion. The thesis statement anchors the portfolio and provides the scaffolding for the pieces of evidence such as written products, tests, video recordings, artwork and journals. The thesis answers the questions of what the student has learned, found meaningful and will implement as life-long learners. The descriptions and analysis of each piece of work could also include a reflection of their learning experience. Finally, the brief analytic descriptions are linked to the conclusion. In the portfolio conclusion, students' learning and future directions for further development are summarized.

## Conclusion

Students gain satisfaction from their own efforts when they are more careful and evaluative of their work. After students examine several writing drafts, they are able to see their growth as a writer. When students put together a portfolio, teachers communicate through clear learning objectives and criteria. Then students select what goes into their portfolio by following criteria to define quality performance. A portfolio with student reflections about how they feel about their work, learning environment and themselves provides a basis for communication to teachers and parents.

Finally, portfolios serve as evidence of learning to parents, school administrators and teachers. So the next time I invite my students to a buffet and want to know which nutritious foods they ate, I could ask them to complete a portfolio. It could consist of a test showing their awareness of the food triangle, a checklist of what and how much they ate at the buffet, a concept map on food and a reflective essay on how they felt about choosing nutritious food to eat.

## References

Gardner, H. (1991). *The unschooled mind: How children think and how schools should teach.* New York: Basic Books.

Helm, J., Beneke, S., & Steinheimer, K. (1998). *Windows on learning: Document young children's work.* New York: Teachers College Press.

Howard, P. (1994). *The owner's manual for the brain.* Austin, TX: Leornian Press.

Perkins, D., & Blythe, T. (1994). Putting understanding up front. *Educational Leadership, 51*(5), 4-7.

Stiggins, R. J. (1997). *The role of portfolios in the communication process: Student-Centered Classroom Assessment* (2nd Ed.). New Jersey: Prentice-Hall, Inc.

http://electronicportfolios.com (accessed Nov 2001)

## About the Author

**Rosalind Mau**, Ph D, taught courses and workshops on assessment and evaluation in the United States, Hong Kong and Singapore. Her most recent work was with heads of departments and subject/level heads in primary and secondary schools in Singapore. Her focus was on alternative assessments, including the use of portfolios. E-mail: rosalindmau@hotmail.com.

# Epilogue

*Mary Cherian and Rosalind Y. Mau*

In our prologue, we likened cruising through this book to riding in a taxi on the Pan Island Expressway (PIE) from one end of Singapore to another. Both the taxi driver and the chapter authors take you on journeys and along the way, tell stories and point out scenes. Because each of us can only guess what it is like to be in another setting, the stories and scenes help us make connections. However, there are key differences. For one thing, the taxi driver's task is to get us from one point to another. The conversation is spontaneous and incidental: to entertain, to amuse, to impress, and perhaps even to educate to some extent. In contrast, our chapter authors have key points they wish to make. The scenes and stories in the chapters have been carefully selected and strategically inserted to illustrate these significant points. The chapter authors' stories and scenes may also entertain, amuse or impress but they serve the greater purpose of communicating about professional practices and ideals.

Writing the paragraphs may have taken each author only minutes but embodied in those paragraphs are years of thinking. The decisions about what is shared have everything to do with this book being written for teachers and teacher educators. Insights on teaching and learning in large classes are shared within these pages so that all of us may grow in the process. This has certainly been true for us, Mary Cherian and Rosalind Mau, as we worked with the chapter authors over the last 2 years. The time has finally come for us to bring it all together in this epilogue. We do not believe there is one standard formula or recipe that would work for everyone. Rather, we draw your attention to ingredients or factors that have been found to be helpful for large-class teaching. The factors tend to be intimately inter-related. They impact the quality of education.

In some instances, the quality of education is compromised in the effort to include as many children as possible. Overcrowded classrooms, teachers with heavy teaching loads and little preparation time or resources, children channeled through schools in an assembly-line fashion—these are at times the sober outcomes. In contrast, the scenarios in this book showcase exemplary practices. However, we must bear in mind that in many large countries in particular, school conditions vary dramatically from region to region and even within the same city. For instance, the Indian classes described in Chapter 3 are in 'middle class' schools in Mumbai. In the same city, there are schools where overcrowding is a reality. Similarly, Beijing (chap. 2) is China's capital and the education centre. Cheng Yuanshan and Rosalind Mau tell us that conditions are not so ideal in remote districts and rural areas of China. But with good leadership, such scenarios can be changed. For some schools to improve, so many of the inter-related factors would need to be changed that only a total transformation would help. Bill Holderness (chap. 1) and Hanna Shachar (chap. 5) were each instrumental in such transformations. The schools they worked with improved not only the quality of education but also the quality of life for children and adults in their school communities.

## Physical Facilities Matter

In many parts of the world, including the inner cities of affluent countries, schools are housed in poorly maintained, overcrowded buildings. Poor physical facilities handicap good teaching and affect the morale of teachers and students. Improving physical facilities is a good way to begin transforming schools. It may seem more logical to start school improvement exercises with the curriculum but in reality, starting with the school building as a launching pad also works well because the building is tangible and not abstract. The outcomes are visible. A palpable sense of celebration comes through as Bill Holderness (chap. 1) recounts how schools worked with local communities to transform overcrowded and under-resourced classrooms in badly neglected school buildings. Improving the physical environment was only one part of the change process but it brought people together and set the stage for changes in classroom functioning as well. When school administrators, teachers, parents and community leaders come together to discuss the physical facilities, they will inevitably have to examine how the buildings and grounds are to be used. Discussions about space are linked to how lessons are conducted, what materials and equipment are needed and all else that is part of the ideal school scenario in each participant's mind. Such exercises have the potential to jump-start thinking about deeper teaching and learning issues. In some cases, the planning may not move beyond the physical facility. This is unfortunate but even in such cases, a physical make-over has the power to uplift spirits and revive morale.

## Teachers are Central

A resounding message throughout the book is that teachers' attitudes, knowledge and skills make a critical difference in large-class teaching. Being trusted and respected by students strengthen the teachers in their role as authority figures who guide and scaffold learning. It is an added advantage when the teaching profession is upheld and respected by the larger community as, for example, in India (chap. 3). Traditionally, in many other parts of the world as well, teachers were held in high esteem. Today, the teaching profession has a status that is elevated but discounted. The desire to become a teacher is considered a high calling. However, the salaries and benefits do not reflect society's recognition of the profession as one that needs complex skills and knowledge.

Regardless of society's image of the teaching profession, the individual teacher has to earn trust and credibility through day-to-day life in the classroom. To this end, good pre-service teacher preparation and ongoing professional development are crucial. The key responsibility for preparing pre-service teachers for large-class teaching rests with the local teacher education institutes. As Bill Holderness (chap. 1) suggests, teacher educators should use effective large-class teaching strategies to model them for their pre-service teachers.

Beijing's (chap. 2) pre-service training procedures illustrate an intensive effort to make sure that important concepts about teaching and learning are understood and internalized before graduating as a teacher. Each teacher trainee prepares and teaches a lesson to peers, gets feedback from peers and supervisors, improves the plan and repeats the cycle until the lesson meets all set criteria. Only then may the trainee deliver the lesson to a 'real' classroom of students. These trainees also have ample opportunities to observe master teachers in action. As a result, graduating teachers are competent in teaching large classes.

## Teachers Need Support

Due partly to the sheer numbers of students in their classes, teachers can feel very alone. Team teaching can make a difference. Hanna Shachar (chap.5) introduced team teaching as part of the new model of instruction in one of the schools in Israel. An advantage of team teaching is that teachers work in teams to synergize teaching strategies for large classes.

Whether teachers are teaching solo in their large classes or team teaching, they need collegial support and encouragement from administrators and staff. In the rural, isolated schools in South Africa, 'by putting neighbouring schools in contact with each other, new possibilities were suddenly created' (chap. 1, p. 6) as teachers shared techniques and gave emotional support and encouragement to each other. Bill Holderness stresses that endorsement and tangible support by the ministry of education are crucial to making feasible teacher meetings and network building. This is the case in Beijing (chap. 2) where the authorities explicitly encouraged teachers to collaborate by sharing ideas and resources and by planning lessons together. Going one step further, every Waldorf School (chap. 4) has a College of Teachers where teachers receive support from their colleagues.

Technology supports the work of teachers. Jessica Ball's (chap. 6) 3rd project involving several African nations illustrates the creative use of technology. Electronic student portfolios (chap. 11) are another example of the usefulness of technology in the hands of competent teachers. Research tells us that teachers who favour constructivist methods shift from using only teacher-directed instruction to more constructivist pedagogy when their classrooms are equipped with computers for the students (Windschitl & Sahl, 2002). Such set-ups may appear to be remote probabilities to some but worldwide initiatives such as UNESCO's *Learning without Frontiers* (UNESCO, 1995) are resulting in rapid changes in the use of technology for education. Computers are clearly part of the solution to supporting individualized teaching and learning for large numbers of students.

## Infrastructures for Efficiency

With large classes, it is important to establish infrastructures for efficiency. Pong and Pallas (2001) found that in virtually every country they studied and regardless of class size, teachers reported whole-class direct instruction most frequently, followed by class discussion. Done well, direct instruction is an effective delivery mode. However, many teachers also resort to direct instruction only because they feel ill equipped to handle small-group and other participatory processes. They rely solely on direct instruction in the name of efficiency. Yet, you would have noticed how frequently group work is mentioned in our chapters as being both viable and desirable for large classes.

Being prepared and organised helps. Well-conceptualised lesson plans; learning materials ready to be distributed; clearly written instructions for group work—these and other preparations enable teachers to introduce exciting activities in large classes. During class, smooth streamlined transitions are necessary. George Jacobs and Loh Wan Inn (chap. 10) recommend specific techniques that make it feasible for a large class of students and their teacher to work together as a cooperative community. These techniques enable smooth transitions. Directions about moving from whole-class to small-group seating arrangements need to be thought through so that the transitions are possible with fluid, non-disruptive moves. Once these transitions become routine, they save a great deal of time.

David Mitchell, an education consultant, observed large classes in Japan and was amazed at how little time it took the students to transition from whole-class seating arrangements to small-group ones (Mitchell, 2001). In the Waldorf Schools, movements involving whole group configurations are common as so much of the school day involves music, movement and the arts. But it takes more than a set of well-rehearsed techniques to have a community of teachers and learners working together in harmony. In the final analysis, it is the relationships within the classroom community that make the difference. Richard Blunt (chap. 4) explains that '...the teacher leads the class, directing the children not with force but through the strength of relationships they establish with them' (p. 59). Teaching large classes well requires reaching and connecting with all the children.

## Reaching and Connecting with Every Student

In very large classes, getting to know every student can be a daunting challenge indeed. Knowing the names of students, greeting students as they enter the classroom and other strategies build teacher-student relationships. Even assessment tools have the potential to provide windows through which teachers may see glimpses of otherwise hidden strengths and vulnerabilities of students. Rosalind Mau (chap. 10) suggests that we get to know students better through portfolio assessments. Student portfolios enable teachers of large classes to get to know quieter, less attention-seeking students who risk being overlooked because, as Doris Martin (chap. 9) points out, 'getting to know students who are reticent requires more effort and patience on the teacher's part' (p.13). Because of the richness of portfolio contents, portfolio assessment can be used to guide planning for children with disabilities and highly able children. However, portfolios alone will not do. Teachers should dialogue with their students through ongoing conversations about their learning and achievements (Hargreaves, Earl & Schmidt, 2002). Thana Thaver (chap. 8), writing about highly able children, sums it up for all children with special needs: 'ultimately (it is) the effectiveness of their teachers and the willingness to make provisions for them in the classroom' (p. 121).

One of the schools in Hanna Shachar's Chapter 5 made more time for teachers to strengthen their relationships with students. The innovations included dramatically revamping the typical school day into one that reduced whole-class teaching time and introduced research in the community. Strategic planning began with the clear and strong conviction that the relationship between teachers and their students was 'the basic foundation of the educational process, without which no improvement in school functioning could be achieved' (chap. 5, p. 87). Teachers must be at the helm, establishing and sustaining teacher-student relationships and a class culture that is conducive to teaching and learning. But the responsibility should not lie exclusively with teachers. Teachers and students must share the responsibility for teaching and learning.

## Teachers and Students Share Responsibility

In the 1960s, UNESCO set up an international commission to look at how we can prepare future generations for a world that is changing more and more rapidly. This commission strongly recommended that education must enable every person 'to solve his own problems, make his own decisions and shoulder his own responsibilities' (UNESCO, 1971). Our efforts are aligned with this recommendation when we, as teachers, share the responsibility for teaching and learning with children in our classes. Delegating certain duties to children provides opportunities for them to shoulder basic responsibilities. Whether it is through peer tutoring, handing out and collecting homework or any of a number of other ways, children can be encouraged to take greater ownership of the teaching and learning in their classes. Hanna Shachar (chap. 5) writes about school reform that introduced students choosing their own topics for research and having to assume responsibility for the research itself. A key principle guiding Jessica Ball's (chap. 6) generative curriculum approach is that students identify some of the curricular content, choose some of the activities and participate in some of the assessments of their own learning. In these two chapters, we see new frontiers of education: unfettered thinking and bold innovations that will prepare today's students for tomorrow's world.

Twenty-five years after the first UNESCO commission on preparing future generations through education, UNESCO set up a second commission with the same purpose. Over the 25 years, the world had changed rapidly. The Cold War was over. In this context, this second commission emphasized the need for 'learning to live together, learning to live with others' (UNESCO, 1996). Today, with international terrorism constantly in the news, this second commission's call is even more urgent. Children need to learn to live together, caring for each other despite differences.

## Children Caring for Children

George Jacobs and Loh Wan Inn (chap. 10) urge us to 'imagine the world we are hoping to foster from within our classrooms...a world in which people collaborate for the welfare of all' (p. 143). To this end, the concepts and techniques of cooperative learning directly enhance student-student interaction. The ethos of cooperative learning is compatible with inclusion, which has as its ultimate vision: 'caring and welcoming communities for all within society' (chap. 7, p. 103). An inclusive school is one where activities are designed such that all can take part. Richard Blunt's (chap. 4) depiction of the Waldorf schools reflects such inclusiveness. The boy with a history of aggression was placed directly in a large class and the teacher 'focused on leading the class through activities that would help him to express his repressed feelings' (p. 45) rather than excluding the child or singling him out. Competent teachers who understand children are able to form caring, inclusive classroom communities where interdependence is the norm.

In their chapter on inclusion, Levan Lim and his co-authors write about the value of peer-mediated strategies (where peers tutor, instruct and help each other in many ways). Similarly, Hanna Shachar found that more positive multi-age relationships resulted when 9th-grade students taught 7th-grade students computer lessons. These ways of working give students opportunities to experience interdependence. As valuable is a community's implicit expectation that children help each other spontaneously: as when students in Lesotho pushed their classmate to school in a wheelbarrow (chap. 7); and older children look out for their younger siblings and friends in the after-school rush home in Mumbai (chap. 3).

## Making Education Pertinent

Thus far, our epilogue has focused on the teacher, the student, the processes and the infrastructures of schools. It goes without saying that the content—the curriculum—matters. What should students learn? Who decides what they should learn? How do we make education pertinent to the learner? Jessica Ball (chap. 6) writes about the value of providing learning opportunities that enable students and teachers to benefit from both established mainstream knowledge bases as well as indigenous knowledge from non-traditional sources. Making education pertinent to students requires that teachers learn to listen and to be open to others' perspectives about what should be learnt, from whom and how. The chances of perceiving the curriculum as pertinent are higher when students are party to decisions about the curriculum.

As one of the instructors who worked with Jessica Ball in Generative Curriculum Model said, "Instructors need to be self-critical and willing to jettison the 'excess baggage' of their own mainstream training and their own cultural blinders" (chap. 6, p. 92).

## Getting off the Expressway

*Teaching Large Classes* has led to one discovery after another for the two of us. We find that there is always something new to learn even about schools in places that are familiar to us. We hope the same has been true for you, the reader. And now, the journey is about to end. What next? We encourage you not to be satisfied by reading about schools and their communities in other parts of the world. To experience large classes elsewhere, seek opportunities to step into them. Spend time just being there, soaking in the ambiance. And it may very well be as rewarding as if we were to stop midway on our journey on the Pan Island Expressway, alight from the taxi and venture into a forested thicket to experience the wonders therein.

# References

Hargreaves, A., Earl, L., & Schmidt, M. (2002). Perspectives on alternative assessment reform. *American Educational Research Journal, 39* (1), 69-95.

Mitchell, D. (2001). *Japanese schools' accomodation to student diversity.* Paper presented at the Specialised Education Seminar Series, National Institute of Education, Nanyang Technological University, Singapore.

Pong, S., & Pallas, A. (2001). Class size and eighth-grade math achievement in the United States and abroad. *Educational evaluation and policy analysis, 23*(3), 251-273.

UNESCO (1971). *Learning to be.* Report of the International Commission on Education for the Twenty-first Century. Paris: Author.

UNESCO (1995). *50 years of education.* Paris: Author. Retrieved March 2, 2002, from http://www.unesco.org/education/educprog/50y/brochure.htm.

UNESCO (1996). *Learning: The treasure within.* Report of the International Commission on Education for the Twenty-first Century. Paris: Author.

Windschitl, M., & Sahl, K. (2002). Tracing teachers' use of technology in a laptop computer school: The interplay of teacher beliefs, social dynamics, and institutional culture. *American Educational Research Journal, 39* (1), 165-205.

# About the Editors

**Mary Cherian**, Ph D, is an educator and child development specialist. She grew up in Singapore where large classes were part of her school experience. Her early work was with individuals with disabilities in Singapore and Chennai, India. She has also taught at the preschool and secondary levels. After completing her Ph D in the United States, she stayed on as an assistant professor at the Virginia Polytechnic Institute and State University. In 1994, she returned to Singapore to head the research and planning division of the National Council of Social Service. While working on this book, she was an assistant professor at the National Institute of Education, Nanyang Technological University, Singapore. E-mail: marycherian_sg@yahoo.com.sg.

**Rosalind Y. Mau**, Ph D, is an educational consultant and writer who taught in the United States, Singapore, Hong Kong and Samoa. She taught multicultural education in the College of Education at the University of Hawaii and later was an associate professor at the National Institute of Education, Nanyang Technological University in Singapore. There she worked with school department heads, vice-principals and principals on teaching, learning and assessment of students in large classes. E-mail: rosalindmau@hotmail.com.

# Index

Page numbers in **bold** print refer to main entries